$\mathcal{P}$resented to:

Mom

$\mathcal{P}$resented by:

Robin

$\mathcal{D}$ate:

Mothers Day - May 10, 1999

GOD'S LITTLE
DEVOTIONAL BOOK
FOR WOMEN

Special Gift Edition

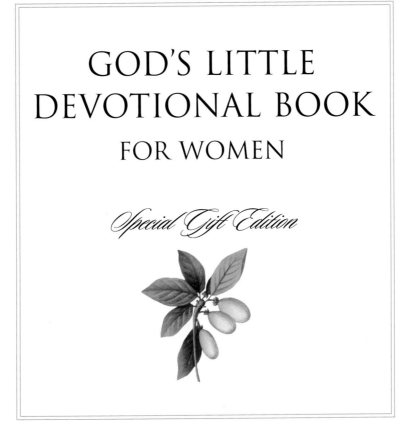

Honor Books
Tulsa, Oklahoma

God's Little Devotional Book for Women - *Special Gift Edition*
ISBN 1-56292-529-6
Copyright ©1998 by Honor Books
P.O. Box 55388
Tulsa, Oklahoma 74155

Devotions drawn from *God's Little Devotional Book for Women*; manuscript prepared by W. B. Freeman Concepts, Inc., Tulsa, Oklahoma.

Introduction

ONE of the primary things most women long for today is time—time to rest, relax, and reflect. Often, just a few minutes spent with a good book can refresh and energize you to go on with the remainder of your day. The demands of running a home, caring for a family, and holding down a job can leave you feeling drained—depleted of all mental, emotional, and spiritual resources. Even if you don't work outside the home, your day is action-packed—transporting kids, running errands, and volunteering anywhere and everywhere. Life seems to go at a faster and faster pace all the time.

To maintain your sanity, you must determine to take breaks—pauses to fill up your body, mind, and spirit with nourishment. While this book can't feed your body, it can feed your mind and your spirit with quotes, scriptures, and stories selected to encourage and challenge you in your daily walk.

The devotions you will find in this better-than-ever version of the best-selling *God's Little Devotional Book for Women* will inspire you with motivating messages and captivating artwork. So get in your favorite chair, with your favorite snack, and your new favorite book—*God's Little Devotional Book for Women - Special Gift Edition*. You'll be glad you did!

My job is to take care of the possible and trust God with the impossible.

6

AS she crept up a hill with eight cars in front of her, Dr. Amanda Whitworth was frustrated. They were stuck behind a slow-moving truck, and she was in a hurry. Amanda's last patient had needed some extra attention, and she was late leaving to pick up her daughter from day school. Now she prayed that she would not be late again. It would be her third time, and because the day school did not tolerate parental tardiness, she would have to make new arrangements for Allie's afternoon care.

Amanda silently fumed at the creeping truck. No one dared pass him on the long hill, since it was impossible to see oncoming cars. Suddenly, the truck driver waved his hand indicating that all was clear. As Amanda zipped past him, it occurred to her that this man was probably a stranger to all who passed him—yet nine people trusted their lives and the lives of their families to him.

In much the same way, we do all we can do, and then we must trust even the smallest details of our lives to the care of God—our loving Heavenly Father. How comforting to know He can always see what's ahead!

And they that know thy name will put their trust in thee: for thou, LORD, hast not forsaken them that seek thee.

Psalm 9:10

You are never so high as when you are on your knees.

ON a stormy day, with two well-experienced guides, a woman climbed the Weisshorn in the Swiss Alps. As they neared the peak, the woman—exhilarated by the view before her—sprang forward and was almost blown away by a gust of wind. One of the guides caught her and pulled her down, saying, "On your knees, madam! You are safe here only on your knees."

We typically regard kneeling as the standard position for prayer, but talking to God isn't limited to a particular position. He can always hear us.

Three women were talking once about the "best" positions for prayer. One argued the importance of holding one's hands together and pointing them upward. The second advocated that prayer was best when one was stretched out on the floor. The third thought standing was better than kneeling. As they talked, a repairman working on a nearby phone system overheard their conversation. Finally, he could contain himself no longer and interjected, "I have found that the most powerful prayer I ever made was while I was dangling upside down from a pole, suspended forty feet above the ground."

The important thing is not your position of prayer, but that you pray!

Humble yourselves in the sight of the Lord, and he shall lift you up.
— *James 4:10* —

*Give your troubles to God:
He will be up all night anyway.*

LEONARD Ravenhill once said about prayer, "One might estimate the weight of the world, tell the size of the celestial city, count the stars of heaven, measure the speed of lightning, and tell the time of the rising and the setting of the sun—but you cannot estimate prayer power. Prayer is as vast as God because He is behind it. Prayer is as mighty as God because He has committed Himself to answer it."

A sign in a cotton factory read: "If your threads get tangled, send for the foreman." One day a new worker got her threads tangled. The more she tried to disentangle them, the worse the situation grew. Finally, she sent for the foreman. He asked, "Why didn't you send for me earlier?" She replied, "I was doing my best." He answered, "No, your best would have been to send for me."

When we face a tough situation, our first response should be to ask for God's help. Prayer opens up the floodgates of God's infinite grace and power. He can act without our prayers, but He chooses to operate within the boundaries of human will and invitation. God wants to help you—just ask Him.

He will not allow your foot to slip;
He who keeps you will not slumber.
Psalm 121:3 NASB

There never was a person who did anything worth doing that did not receive more than he gave.

MOST authorities believe King Solomon's Temple was built on Mount Moriah, the place where Abraham was told to sacrifice Isaac. There's a Hebrew legend, however, that presents a different story.

The legend says that two brothers lived on adjoining farms which were divided from the peak to the base of the mountain. The younger brother lived alone. The older brother had a large family.

One night during harvest, the older brother awoke and thought, *My brother is all alone. To cheer his heart, I will take some of my sheaves and lay them on his side of the field.*

At the same hour, the younger brother awoke and thought, *My brother has a large family and greater needs than I. As he sleeps, I'll put some of my sheaves on his side of the field.* Each brother went out carrying his sheaves to the other's field. Halfway across, they bumped into one another in the dark. When they told each other what they were doing, they dropped their sheaves and embraced. It is at that place, the legend claims, the Temple was built.

This story exemplifies the best expression of love—*giving*. Giving is one of life's best relationship-builders.

For God so loved the world, that he gave his only begotten Son, that whosoever believeth in him should not perish, but have everlasting life.
John 3:16

What sunshine is to flowers, smiles are to humanity. They are but trifles, to be sure but, scattered along life's pathway, the good they do is inconceivable.

14

THE practice of one particular church was to dismiss the children from the Sunday morning services just prior to the sermon. The children would all march forward in a makeshift processional and sing a song as they passed the pulpit on their way to hear a special sermon prepared just for them. The pastor greatly enjoyed this part of the service. He made it a point to smile at each child and always hoped to receive a smile in return.

One morning, to his surprise, a curly-headed four-year-old girl ran out of the procession and threw herself into her mother's arms, sobbing deeply. After the service, the pastor sought out the mother to see what had happened. The child had told her, "I smiled at God, but He didn't smile back."

The pastor's heart sank. He had failed to smile, and her joy had turned to anguish.

We may think something as simple as a smile couldn't possibly represent God to those around us, but we can touch someone's life through our smile. Genuine smiles are a sign of affirmation, appreciation, and love.

We always feel better when we smile. Remember, when you smile at someone, they usually smile back.

A happy heart makes the face cheerful.
Proverbs 15:13 NIV

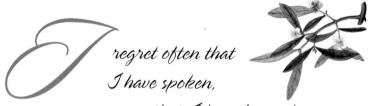

*I regret often that
I have spoken,
never that I have been silent.*

16

WHEN Western Union asked Thomas Edison to name his price for the "ticker" he had invented, he asked for several days to consider it. His wife suggested $20,000, but he thought such an amount was exorbitant.

At the appointed time, he went to the meeting still unsure about his price. When the official asked, "How much?" Edison tried to say $20,000, but the words just wouldn't come out of his mouth. The official finally broke the silence and asked, "Well, how about $100,000?"

Silence often allows others to say something better than we could have said ourselves! When we keep quiet, others have a greater interest in our thoughts. When we have an interested audience, our words have greater impact.

The Bible tells us that even a fool may be thought wise when he keeps his mouth shut. (Proverbs 17:28.) Silence can keep us from embarrassing ourselves. People may think we are smarter than we really are!

When you feel you must speak, weigh the impact of your words and keep this thought in mind, "The *less* said, the *best* said." We can't get in trouble for what we don't say! Like Edison, we might even benefit from our silence.

In the multitude of words there wanteth not sin: but he that refraineth his lips is wise.

Proverbs 10:19

*W*orry is like a rocking chair:
It gives you something to do,
but doesn't get you anywhere.

18

PEOPLE who continually worry about every detail of their lives are like a patient in a mental hospital who stood with her ear pressed against the wall.

"What are you doing?" asked an attendant.

"Shhhh," the woman whispered, beckoning the attendant to join her at the wall.

The attendant pressed her ear to the wall and stood there for several moments listening. "I can't hear anything," she said.

"I know," the patient replied with a furrowed brow. "It's been like that all day!"

Some worry about what might be said. Others worry about what hasn't been said. Some worry what might happen. Others worry about what hasn't happened that should have happened by now. Some worry about their future, while others fret over the consequences of their past.

Worry produces nothing. In fact, worry is counterproductive. It ties up your mental resources and depletes your physical energy. It cuts you off from spiritual refreshment and hinders your creativity.

We were created to live prosperous lives in our mind, our body, and our spirit. Like a flower we were meant to blossom, not to wither on the vine. Put Jesus in charge of your worries today, and walk in abundant life!

Casting the whole of your care [all your anxieties, all your worries, all your concerns, once and for all] on Him, for He cares for you affectionately and cares about you watchfully.

1 Peter 5:7 AMP

*L*ook around you and be distressed,

look within you and be depressed,

look to *J*esus and be at rest.

20

THE 911 emergency system has amazing capabilities. In most places in the United States, a person need only dial those three numbers to be instantly connected to a dispatcher. The dispatcher immediately sees on a computer screen the caller's telephone number, address, and the name under which the number is listed. Also listening in on the call are police, fire, and paramedic assistants. A caller does not even have to say anything once the call is made. Even rasping coughs and hysterical cries have brought a quick response. The dispatcher knows where the call is coming from, and help is sent.

At times, situations in our lives are so desperate and our pain so deep we can only muster 911 prayers to God. These "SOS" prayers often use the same words a person would use when calling 911: "God, I need help!" God hears each one. He knows our name and every detail of the situation. Like a heavenly dispatcher, He will send precisely what is needed to assist us.

Also like a 911 dispatcher, our Heavenly Dispatcher may have some advice to sustain us through a crisis. Keep a listening ear and remember, help is on the way!

In my distress I cried unto the LORD, and he heard me.
Psalm 120:1

*Daily prayers will
diminish your cares.*

MANY children learn to count on their fingers, but a nurse once taught a child to pray on his fingers.

Your thumb is nearest to your heart, so first pray for those who are closest to you. Your own needs should be included, as well as those of your family and friends.

The second finger is used for pointing. Pray for those who point you toward the truth. Pray for your teachers, mentors, pastors, and all those who inspire your faith.

The third finger is the tallest. Let it stand for the leaders in every sphere of life. Pray for those in authority—both within the body of Christ and those who hold offices in various areas of government.

The fourth finger is the weakest, as every pianist knows. Let it stand for those who are in trouble and pain—the sick or abused.

The fifth finger is the smallest. Let it stand for those who often go unnoticed, including those who suffer loneliness and deprivation.

Use this simple and wonderful reminder in your own daily prayers, and your own daily cares will fade into the background as you give your needs to God and concentrate on the needs of others.

Evening, and morning, and at noon, will I pray,
and cry aloud: and he shall hear my voice.
Psalm 55:17

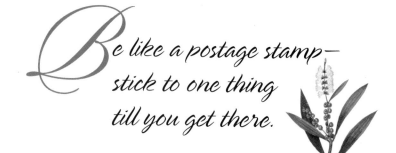

Be like a postage stamp—stick to one thing till you get there.

ALL her life, Veronica worked in jobs that served other people but gave her little personal satisfaction. As a young girl, she missed a great deal of school to take care of her younger siblings and help with the family business. Consequently, she never learned to read.

After marrying, she worked as a cook, memorizing ingredient labels and recipes to conceal her illiteracy. Every day she lived in fear of making a mistake, while dreaming of one day being able to read.

Then, a serious illness put Veronica in the hospital. When she left the hospital, she had a long recovery at home. Her health improved, but not enough for her to go back to work. She saw this time as her opportunity to learn to read and enrolled in an adult reading program.

Veronica's new reading skills boosted her confidence, and she became involved in her church and in organizing community activities. She wrote a prize-winning cookbook and became a local celebrity.

Veronica never let go of her dream while working hard wherever she found herself. In the end, her dreams were realized far beyond her imagination!

Never let go of your dreams—keep working until you get there!

Be steadfast, immovable, always abounding in the work of the Lord, knowing that your toil is not in vain in the Lord.
1 Corinthians 15:58 NASB

A good laugh is sunshine in a house.

26

PEGGY was nervous about the upcoming dinner party she and her husband were hosting. It was their first time to have dinner guests since the birth of their son, Pete. Adding to Peggy's tension was the fact that one of the guests was her husband's new supervisor.

Sensing the tension in his parents, the baby became irritable and fussy the day of the dinner party, which only added to Peggy's frustration. In an attempt to comfort little Pete, Peggy picked him up, raised him high over her head, and kissed his bare tummy. To her surprise, he smiled and giggled—the first genuine laugh she had heard from him.

In an instant, the evening took on an entirely new tenor. Peggy relaxed, and Baby Pete relaxed as well. The dinner party was a great success.

Can the laughter of a little child change a day? Absolutely! So also can the laughter shared between two adults or the chuckle prompted by the memory of a funny event.

When you're feeling frustrated or stressed, don't allow yourself to explode in anger. Get alone if you have to, but find a reason to laugh, and watch the stress melt away!

The light in the eyes [of him whose heart is joyful]
rejoices the hearts of others.
Proverbs 15:30 AMP

Each loving act says loud and clear, "I love you. God loves you. I care. God cares."

A warm-from-the-oven casserole taken to the home of a sick friend.

A bouquet of flowers from your garden given to a new neighbor.

A thank-you note sent to the performers who did such

an excellent job during a concert or play you attended.

A loaf of freshly baked cinnamon bread brought

to the office for coffee break.

A box of cookies taken to the police station on Christmas day

to encourage those who are on duty during the holiday.

An invitation to a bachelor to join your family for a home-cooked meal.

A note of appreciation sent to your child's coach or teacher.

A smile for a discouraged person in the grocery store checkout line.

A call to ask with genuine care and concern, "How are you doing?"

A candy bar left in a co-worker's mail slot.

We may not think of these as acts of Christian witnessing, yet they are. *Every* act of loving-kindness reflects God's loving-kindness for His people. We give because Jesus Christ has so freely given His love to us. He is the example we follow.

Never dismiss an act of loving-kindness as being too small or inconsequential. God will magnify even our smallest deeds to reveal His love to others.

*Beloved, let us love one another: for love is of God;
and every one that loveth is born of God. . . . for God is love.*

1 John 4:7-8

A good deed is never lost;
he who sows courtesy reaps friendship,
and he who plants kindness gathers love.

JOY Sprague knows how to brighten the days of her customers. As the postmaster for Little Cranberry Island, Maine, she actually has customers competing to get their pictures on the post-office wall. Every twenty-fifth customer to use the U.S. Postal Service's Express Mail is a winner. Their picture is taken, then hung on the wall (which is actually a portion of the general store); and they are given a plate of Joy's home-baked cream puffs!

That's not all Joy does to make Little Cranberry, population ninety, a friendlier place. She operates a mail-order stamp business that is so popular her tiny post office ranks fourth in sales out of 450 outlets in Maine. Why? Most of Joy's customers are summer visitors who want to stay up-to-date with island news. Along with each order, Joy sends a snapshot of an island scene and a handwritten note about island events. One of the residents has remarked, "She invents ways to bring pleasure to others."

Why not ask the Lord to give you creative ideas which will brighten someone's life today. Perhaps a brief telephone call or post card will remind them how important they really are to you and to God, their Heavenly Father.

Let us not be weary in well doing: for in due season we shall reap, if we faint not.

Galatians 6:9

*K*ind words can be short and easy to speak
but their echoes are truly endless.

MANY years ago a famous singer was contacted to perform at a Paris opera house. The event was sold out in a matter of days. The entire city was abuzz with anticipation. The night of the performance, the hall was packed with stately dressed men and women eager to hear the much-admired musician. Then, the house manager took the stage and announced, "Ladies and gentlemen, thank you for your enthusiastic support. I am afraid that due to illness, the woman whom you've all come to hear will not be performing tonight. However, we have found a suitable substitute we hope will provide you with comparable entertainment."

The crowd voiced its disappointment so loudly that few heard the singer's name. Frustration replaced the former excitement. The stand-in singer gave everything she had, but when her performance was over she was met with an uncomfortable silence rather than applause. Then, from the balcony, a child stood up and shouted, "Mommy, I think you are wonderful!"

The crowd immediately responded with a thunderous ovation.

Once in a while we each need to hear someone say, "I think you are wonderful." Why not be the person who gives that kind word of encouragement to another today?

She opens her mouth with skillful and godly Wisdom, and on her tongue is the law of kindness [giving counsel and instruction].
Proverbs 31:26 AMP

*Nothing beats love at
first sight except love
with insight.*

TWO lifelong friends in their early fifties began to argue over the upcoming marriage of one of them to a man who was only in his thirties.

"I just don't believe in May-December marriages," the friend said. "After all, December is going to find in May the strength and virility of springtime, but whatever is May going to find in December?"

The bride-to-be thought for a moment and then replied with a twinkle in her eye, "Christmas."

Many couples who claim they fell in love at first sight look back after years of marriage, and what they thought was love was really something else. "I was just infatuated," they say. Or, "We felt an instant attraction to one another." Or, "There was electricity between us." Love, however, is a word they have come to cherish. It is something they now share that is far richer and more meaningful than the emotions they felt in the beginning.

One of the great qualities about genuine love is that it grows and deepens over time. Time is life's nursery for love. Tend to it as you would your most cherished plant, and the fragrance of love's bloom will continually remain.

Determination to be wise is the first step toward becoming wise! And with your wisdom, develop common sense and good judgment.

Proverbs 4:7 TLB

The best way to hold a man is in your arms.

36

THIS old childhood rhyme is one that many people remember:

> Kiss and hug,
> Kiss and hug,
> Kiss your sweetie,
> On the mug.

While the rhyme was often used by children in order to ridicule the puppy-love behavior of their older brothers and sisters, the practice of kissing and hugging actually has many healthful benefits beyond those of building a loving relationship.

A West German magazine reported the results of a study conducted by a life insurance company. The researchers discovered that husbands who kiss their wives every morning live an average of five years longer; are involved in fewer automobile accidents; are ill 50 percent less, as noted by sick days; and earn 20 to 30 percent more money.

Other researchers have found that kissing and hugging release endorphins, giving the mind and body a sense of genuine well-being that is directly translated into better health. And the effects of touch—hugs, massage, and pats—on infants and children is well-documented. They eat better, digest their food better, have less trouble falling asleep, and sleep longer periods of time. God created us to touch and be touched!

A kiss a day just may keep the doctor away!

The man should give his wife all that is her right as a married woman, and the wife should do the same for her husband.

1 Corinthians 7:3 TLB

Ninety percent of the friction of daily life is caused by the wrong tone of voice.

38

A DEMANDING wife continually nagged her husband to conform to her very high standards. She insisted every aspect of his life be honed to perfection. Feeling thoroughly whipped, the man finally said, "Why don't you just write it all down? Then you won't have to tell me these things all the time." She gladly complied.

A short time later the wife died. Within the course of a year, the man met another woman and remarried. His new life seemed to be a perpetual honeymoon. He could hardly believe the great joy he was experiencing.

One day he came across the list his first wife had written. He read it and realized, to his amazement, he was following all of the instructions even though his second wife had never mentioned them.

He thought about what might have happened and finally said to a friend, "My former wife began her statements, 'I hate it when. . . ,' but my new wife says, 'I just love it when. . . .'"

Rather than demanding that her husband be the man she expected him to be, the second wife enabled him to be the man God had created him to be. It's amazing what a few little words and a loving tone of voice can do.

A man finds joy in giving an apt reply—
and how good is a timely word!
Proverbs 15:23 NIV

*Forgiveness is giving love
when there is no reason to.*

LISA was shocked when she discovered that David had run up thousands of dollars on their credit cards. Not only was she furious about the mountain of debt, she was frustrated with herself for not recognizing David's compulsive spending habits.

Rather than wait for something to happen, Lisa took two bold steps. The first was to convince David he needed help, and the second was to seek out a financial planner. She learned if she carefully monitored the family funds, they could be out of debt in a few years. This brought hope for their financial future and their marital future.

Another turnaround in their marriage came when David asked Lisa to forgive him. She found that forgiving David freed her to turn away from the matter of money and to focus on their relationship. She decided it was possible to love someone even though they had "messed up." Forgiving made trust possible again, and once trust was reestablished their marriage began to heal.

Forgiveness turns the heart away from what was and is, to what can be. Is it time for you to take some bold steps? If love is your motive, be encouraged! Situations, and people, can change.

Blessed are the merciful, For they shall obtain mercy.
Matthew 5:7 NKJV

Nothing is so strong as gentleness. Nothing is so gentle as real strength.

MENTOR Graham was so absorbed in evaluating assignments he failed to notice the youthful giant who slouched into his Illinois schoolroom one day after school. After his eyes had adjusted to the brightness of the late-afternoon sunshine, he recognized the youth as a newcomer to the community. The lad already had a reputation for "whipping the daylights" out of all the local toughs.

Graham would have been justified in thinking, *What does he want here? Am I in danger?* Instead, he looked up and down the six-foot-four-inches of muscle and ignorance before him and offered to help the lad with his reading. When the young man left the schoolroom an hour later, he had several books under his arm—a loan from Mentor Graham with a promise of more in the future.

Few people remember Graham. He was a quiet man, simply willing to do his best for any student who came his way. His pupil, however, is remembered by many. His name was Abraham Lincoln.

A kind, helpful response to others is often perceived by them as strength. It is this gentle strength to which we are drawn. When you find yourself in a precarious situation, try a gentle touch.

Thou hast also given me the shield of Thy salvation, and Thy right hand upholds me; and Thy gentleness makes me great.

Psalm 18:35 NASB

43

Everyone has patience—
successful people learn to use it.

44

SEVERAL years ago a speedboat driver was in a serious accident. In recounting what had happened, she said that she had been clipping along at top speed when her boat veered just slightly, hitting a wave at a dangerous angle. The combined force of her speed and the size and angle of the wave sent the boat spinning wildly into the air. She was thrown from her seat and thrust so deeply into the water that she could not see any light from the surface. Dazed, she had no idea which direction was up.

Rather than panic, the woman remained calm and waited for the buoyancy of her life vest to begin pulling her up. Then she swam in that direction.

We often find ourselves surrounded by many voices, each with a different opinion, and we simply don't know which way is up. When this happens, we need to exercise patience and spend time with the Lord. We must read His Word, the Bible, and wait for His gentle tug on our hearts to pull us toward His will. The more we read, the more confident we will become, especially when His written Word and that gentle tug on our hearts come into agreement.

But let patience have her perfect work,
that ye may be perfect and entire, wanting nothing.
James 1:4

Watch out for temptation—the more you see of it the better it looks.

AS a teen, Megan arrived home from school just in time to watch an hour of soaps before doing her homework. She enjoyed the escape into the TV world and wasn't really aware that the programs were creating an inordinate amount of sexual curiosity in her. Over months and years of watching the shows, Megan's perspective on life began to shift. She began to think, *Relationships don't need to be pure; in fact, the impure ones seem more exciting. Fidelity doesn't matter, as long as a person is "happy."*

As a college student, Megan found it easy to participate in one-night stands. Then, after a short marriage ended in catastrophe, she sought help from a counselor. At the outset, it was difficult for the counselor to understand why Megan had engaged in extramarital affairs. She had been a model teenager, as far as her public behavior was concerned. Finally, the counselor discovered the source of the temptation that drove Megan to participate in her hidden life.

What we see on TV inevitably becomes a part of our memory bank, forming background information for justifying our behavior. If what you're seeing isn't what you want to do— change the channel!

Keep watching and praying that you may not come into temptation.
Mark 14:38 NASB

It is such a comfort to drop tangles of life into God's hands and leave them there.

48

MANY years ago, a young woman who felt called to the ministry was accepted into seminary. With only two other women enrolled, their very presence seemed to make the male classmates uncomfortable. She felt isolated, yet on display at the same time. To make matters worse, many of her professors were doing their best to destroy her faith, rather than build it up. Even her private devotional time seemed dry and lonely.

At Christmas break she sought her father's counsel. "How can I be strong in my resolve and straight in my theology with all that I face there?"

Her father took a pencil from his pocket and laid it on the palm of his hand. "Can that pencil stand upright by itself?" he asked her.

"No," she replied. Then her father grasped the pencil in his hand and held it in an upright position. "Ah," she said, "but you are holding it now."

"Daughter," he replied, "your life is like this pencil. Jesus Christ is the one who can hold you and keep you upright." The young woman took her pencil and returned to seminary.

When you're facing a difficult situation, remember your Father God is holding you in His hands.

Cast your cares on the LORD and he will sustain you.
Psalm 55:22 NIV

*Friendship improves happiness,
and abates misery, by doubling our joy,
and dividing our grief.*

THEY call themselves the "Ladies of the Lake," but they never set out to be a club. The group began when one of the women returned home exhausted from a business trip and came to the conclusion that she had too much of one thing in her life: MEN! With a husband and two boys at home, a predominately male work environment, and an elderly father and uncle to care for, she resolved to set some time aside for herself and a few female friends.

Over the years, Paula hadn't cultivated very many friendships with other women, but she was determined to see that change. Eventually she discovered three like-minded women. The women pulled out their calendars over dinner one evening and agreed on a schedule—"A trip to the lake at least once a quarter!"

At the lake, the women would listen to classical music, fix gourmet dinners, and enjoy the view from the deck. They would talk for hours, with no agenda.

These types of friendships strengthen us in our various roles as wives, mothers, and employees. Set aside some regular "time with the girls"; you'll always come back to your family recharged and ready to go!

A friend loves at all times, and a brother is born for adversity.
Proverbs 17:17 NIV

*E*veryone has an invisible sign
hanging from his neck saying,
"Make me feel important!"

52

IT isn't enough to say in our hearts
That we like a man for his ways,
It isn't enough that we fill our minds
Nor is it enough that we honor a man
As our confidence upward mounts,
It's going right up to the man himself,
And telling him so that counts!
If a man does a work you really admire,
Don't leave a kind word unsaid,
In fear that to do so might make him vain
And cause him to "lose his head."
But reach out your hand and tell him,
"Well done," and see how his gratitude swells;
It isn't the flowers we strew on the grave,
It's the word to the living that tells.

—Anonymous

When there is a lack of praise, our friends and loved ones
may think we've drawn negative conclusions about them. We
can actually wound others by withholding our praise. Let
someone know you think well of him or her today. Give your
husband, children, and friends specific words of praise today.
Tell them what you love about them. What a difference your
words will make!

Therefore encourage one another and build each other up,
just as in fact you are doing.
1 Thessalonians 5:11 NIV

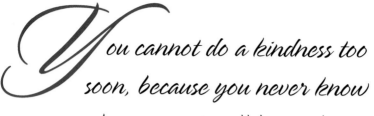

You cannot do a kindness too soon, because you never know how soon it will be too late!

BEFORE being elected the twenty-fifth president of the United States, William McKinley served in Congress. On his way to his congressional office one morning, he boarded a streetcar and took the only remaining seat. Minutes later, a woman who appeared to be ill boarded the car. Unable to find a seat, she clutched an overhead strap next to one of McKinley's colleagues. The other congressman hid behind his newspaper and did not offer the woman his seat. McKinley walked up the aisle, tapped the woman on the shoulder, offered her his seat, and took her place in the aisle.

Years later when McKinley became president, this same congressman was recommended to him for a post as ambassador to a foreign nation. McKinley refused to appoint him. He feared a man who didn't have the courtesy to offer his seat to a sick woman in a crowded streetcar would lack the sensitivity necessary to be an ambassador in a troubled nation. The disappointed congressman bemoaned his fate to many in Washington but never did learn why McKinley chose someone else for the position.

Acts of kindness can lead you to prominence. Then, from your position of prominence, you can be kind to even more people!

But encourage one another day after day,
as long as it is still called "Today."
Hebrews 3:13 NASB

*Stack every bit of criticism between
two layers of praise.*

SHORTLY after graduation, Joe and Lana married. One of their first marital difficulties was their very different understanding of what "being on time" meant. Not wanting to end the honeymoon stage too early, Lana only mildly complained about Joe's being late. But Joe never took the hint, and soon her complaining turned to outright criticism.

On the surface, there may not seem to be much difference between exposing a problem and criticizing, but in a relationship, the right or wrong choice of words can bring very different responses. Criticism attacks someone's personality and character. When Lana criticized Joe, she would say, "You're only thinking about yourself!"

Putting an issue on the table for discussion in a positive manner is the first step toward finding a resolution. A person who asks gently, "Does it embarrass you when we are late?" is opening a dialog for finding the solution to the problem. Criticism only wounds the spirit, puts the other person on the defensive, and usually ends up in a no-resolution argument.

Watch what you say! Criticism can cause a wound that takes years to heal, but a kind, gracious, problem-solving attitude can save you years of tears!

Correct, rebuke and encourage—
with great patience and careful instruction.
2 Timothy 4:2 NIV

In trying times,
don't quit trying.

Bouquet de Camélias Narcisses et Pensées.

P. J. Redouté.   Victor

SOMEBODY said that it couldn't be done,
But he with a chuckle replied,
That "maybe it couldn't" but he would be one
Who wouldn't say so till he'd tried.
So he buckled right in with the trace of a grin
On his face. If he worried, he hid it.
He started to sing as he tackled the thing
That couldn't be done. And he did it.
Somebody scoffed: "Oh, you'll never do that,
At least no one ever has done it."
But he took off his coat and took off his hat
And the first thing he knew he'd begun it.
With the lift of his chin and a bit of a grin,
If any doubt rose he forbid it;
He started to sing as he tackled the thing
That couldn't be done, and he did it.
There are thousands to tell you it cannot be done,
There are thousands to prophesy failure;
There are thousands to point out to you, one by one,
The dangers that wait to assail you,
But just buckle right in with a bit of a grin,
Then take off your coat and go to it.
Just start in to sing as you tackle the thing
That cannot be done, and you'll do it.

—Unknown

And let us not get tired of doing what is right, for after a while we will reap a harvest of blessing if we don't get discouraged and give up.

❧ Galatians 6:9 TLB ☙

59

*To love what you do and feel that it matters—
how could anything be more fun?*

A NEWSPAPER in England once asked this question of its readers, "Who are the happiest people on the earth?"

The four prize-winning answers were:

—A little child building sand castles.

—A craftsman or artist whistling over a job well done.

—A mother, bathing her baby after a busy day.

—A doctor who has finished a difficult and dangerous operation that saved a human life.

The paper's editors were surprised to find that virtually no one submitted kings, emperors, millionaires, or other people of riches or rank as the happiest people on earth.

W. Beran Wolfe once said, "If you observe a really happy man you will find him building a boat, writing a symphony, educating his son, growing double dahlias in his garden, or looking for dinosaur eggs in the Gobi desert. He will not be searching for happiness as if it were a collar button that has rolled under the radiator. He will not be striving for it as a goal in itself. He will have become aware that he is happy in the course of living life twenty-four crowded hours of the day."

You can find happiness in even the most mundane things in life, if you simply choose to have a happy heart.

When you eat the labor of your hands,
You shall be happy, and it shall be well with you.
Psalm 128:2 NKJV

$\mathcal{L}$*ife is a coin.*
You can spend it any way you wish,
but you can only spend it once.

62

ANITA Septimus has worked as a social worker for HIV-infected children since 1985. In the first few months she worked with her tiny clients, three of them died. Despair began to overwhelm her. She made a commitment to stick with the job for three more months, but during that time she could not get a friend's words out of her thoughts, *You have not chosen a pretty profession.*

She had to admit, her friend was right. It took resolve to accept that fact and simply do what she could to help families make the most of what remained of their children's lives. She is still there today.

Over the last ten years, her clinic has grown considerably. Today, Anita and her staff care for more than 300 families with AIDS children. They go into their homes, teach infection prevention, and help the parents plan for the future. The children are regularly taken on trips to the zoo, the circus, and summer camp.

One AIDS baby wasn't expected to see her first birthday, but she recently celebrated her tenth. Such amazing clients give back to Anita what she calls "an indestructible sense of hope"— a precious gift!

For what is your life? It is even a vapor that appears for a little time and then vanishes away.
James 4:14 NKJV

Diligence is the mother of good fortune.

64

GOD'S LITTLE DEVOTIONAL BOOK FOR WOMEN

ON a shelf sits a beautiful and expensive carving from the Orient. It is a statue of a lady wearing a tall headdress, and balanced atop the headdress is an intricately carved ball. Inside that seamless sphere is another slightly smaller sphere of equal intricacy—and inside that still another, and then another until one can no longer see through the tiny carved holes to see how many more balls there actually are.

Several things make this orb truly remarkable. Each of the nested balls is seamless, completely free from the one outside it and inside it, and magnificent in its airy, lacy design. The orb was carved from a single piece of ivory over 100 years ago, before the days of electronic magnifying instruments.

Why did the artist carve so many layers with such precision? The smallest orbs would not be clearly seen by most people, yet each one was finished with as much skill and artistry as was applied to the larger, outer ones.

The small details of a job may not always remain unnoticed or unseen. Like this artist, your excellence in the small things can bring you prosperity in life and leave a legacy for future generations to follow.

The hand of the diligent makes rich.
Proverbs 10:4 NKJV

Courage is resistance to fear,

mastery of fear.

Not the absence of fear.

NAPOLEON called Marshall Ney the bravest man he had ever known. Yet Ney's knees trembled so badly one morning before a battle, he had difficulty mounting his horse. When he was finally in the saddle, he shouted contemptuously down at his limbs, "Shake away, knees. You would shake worse than that if you knew where I am going to take you!"

Courage is not a matter of simply not being afraid. It is a matter of taking action even when you are afraid!

Courage is also more than sheer bravado shouting, "I can do this!" and launching out with a do-or-die attitude over some reckless dare.

True courage is manifested when a person chooses to take a difficult or even dangerous course of action because it is the right thing to do. Courage is looking beyond yourself to what is best for another.

The source of all courage is the Holy Spirit, our Comforter. God has given Him to us to remain at our side to help us. When we welcome Him into our lives and He compels us to do something, we can confidently trust He will be right there with us, helping us get it done!

Therefore, take up the full armor of God,
that you may be able to resist in the evil day, and having
done everything, to stand firm. Stand firm therefore.
Ephesians 6:13-14 NASB

The art of being wise is the art of knowing what to overlook.

THE story is told of a couple at their golden wedding anniversary celebration. Surrounded by her children, grandchildren, and great grandchildren, the wife was asked the secret to a long and happy marriage. With a loving glance toward her husband, she answered: "On my wedding day, I decided to make a list of ten of my husband's faults which, for the sake of our marriage, I would overlook. I figured I could live with at least ten faults."

A guest asked her to identify some of the faults she had chosen to overlook. Her husband looked a bit troubled at the thought of having his foibles and flaws revealed to his progeny. However, his wife sweetly replied, "To tell you the truth, dear, I never did get around to listing them. Instead, every time my husband did something that made me hopping mad, I would simply say to myself, *Lucky for him that's one of the ten!*"

Even the most devoted spouses and friends will experience storms in their relationships from time to time. Some problems are worth addressing in order to resolve them. Others are best left undisclosed. In time, issues of little importance tend to blow past without any need for a "blowup."

A man's wisdom gives him patience; it is to
his glory to overlook an offense.
Proverbs 19:11 NIV

People don't care how much you know, until they know how much you care —about them.

ON a bitter cold Virginia evening, an old man waited on a path by a river, hoping for someone on a horse to carry him across. Anxiously he watched as several horsemen appeared. He let the first pass by without making an effort to get his attention, then another and another. Finally, only one rider remained. As he drew near, the old man caught his eye and asked, "Sir, would you mind giving me a ride to the other side?"

The rider helped the man onto his horse and, sensing he was half-frozen, decided to take him all the way home. As they rode, the horseman asked, "Why didn't you ask one of the other men to help you? I was the last one. What if I had refused?" The old man said, "When I looked into their eyes and saw they had no concern for my condition, I knew it was useless to ask. When I looked into your eyes, I saw kindness."

At the door of the man's house the rider resolved, *May I never get too busy in my own affairs that I fail to respond to the needs of others.* And with that, Thomas Jefferson turned back toward the White House.

And though I have the gift of prophecy, and understand all mysteries, and all knowledge; and though I have all faith, so that I could remove mountains, and have not charity, I am nothing.

1 Corinthians 13:2

I don't know the secret to success but the key to failure is to try to please everyone.

72

THE story is told of a painter who desired to produce one work which would please the entire world. She drew a picture which required her utmost skill and took it to the public marketplace. She posted directions at the bottom of the piece for spectators to mark each portion of the picture that didn't meet their approval. The spectators came and, in general, applauded the work. But each, eager to make a personal critique, marked a small portion of the picture. By evening, the painter was mortified to find the entire picture had become a blot.

The next day the painter returned with a copy of the original picture. This time she asked the spectators to mark the portions of the work they admired. The spectators again complied. When the artist returned several hours later, she found every stroke that had been panned the day before had received praise by this day's critics.

The artist concluded, "I now believe the best way to please one-half of the world is not to mind what the other says."

People will always have an opinion about us. That is why we must live our lives to please God. Then we will not fret over the opinions of others.

No one can serve two masters; for either he will hate the one and love the other, or he will hold to one and despise the other.
Matthew 6:24 NASB

$\mathcal{D}$o not
follow
where the
path may
lead—
go instead
where
there is no
path and
leave a
trail.

74

MANY years ago an intern in a New York hospital heard a surgeon bemoan the fact that most brain tumors were fatal. The surgeon predicted that some day a surgeon would discover how to save the lives of these patients. Intern Ernest Sachs determined to be that surgeon. At the time, the leading expert on the anatomy of the brain was Sir Victor Horsley. Sachs received permission to study under him but felt he should prepare for the experience by spending six months studying under some of the most able physicians in Germany. Then he went to England, where for two years he assisted Dr. Horsley in long and intricate experiments on dozens of monkeys.

When Sachs returned to America he was ridiculed for requesting the opportunity to treat brain tumors. For years he fought obstacles and discouragement, driven by an uncontrollable urge to succeed in his quest. Today, largely thanks to Dr. Sachs, the majority of brain tumors can be cured. His book, *The Diagnosis and Treatment of Brain Tumors*, is considered the standard authority on the subject.

Because something isn't presently done doesn't mean it can't be done. Maybe you are the one to do it!

Your ears shall hear a word behind you, saying,
"This is the way, walk in it."
Isaiah 30:21 NKJV

There is one thing alone that stands the brunt of life throughout its length; a quiet conscience.

PRESIDENT Woodrow Wilson was approached one day by one of his secretaries, who suggested he take off from his work to engage in a particular diversion he enjoyed. President Wilson replied, "My boss won't let me do it."

"Your boss?" the secretary asked, wondering who could be the boss of the chief executive officer of the United States.

"Yes," said Wilson. "I have a conscience that is my boss. It drives me to the task, and will not let me accept this tempting invitation."

Our conscience is one of the most precious things we possess. Through our conscience we receive inner prompting from God which, when we heed its warnings, will point us toward a safe and eternal way.

It has been said, "A conscience is like a thermostat on an air conditioning unit—it kicks in when things are on the verge of getting too hot."

It is possible to ignore our conscience and follow the crowds, but this is a sad waste of our lives. The conscience is the window to the soul through which we hear the voice of God, Who always leads us to success and inner peace.

Listen carefully, He always has something good to say!

If our hearts do not condemn us, we have confidence before God.
1 John 3:21 NIV

77

Expect great things from God.

Attempt great things for God.

GLADYS Aylward saw herself as a simple woman who just did what God called her to do. Yet, her life was so remarkable that both a book (*The Small Woman*) and a movie (*The Inn of Sixth Happiness*) were produced about the great things God accomplished through her.

A British citizen, Aylward left her home in 1920 and sailed for China. There she bought orphans who were being systematically discarded, children who had been displaced by the political upheavals of the time and left to starve or wander on their own until placed in government warehouses. Gladys gave these children a home.

When the Japanese invaded China, she was forced to flee the mainland with 100 children. They ended up on the island of Formosa. There she continued to devote her life to raising children who knew no other mother.

Gladys explains her amazing work for God like this: "I did not choose this. I was led into it by God. I am not really more interested in children than I am in other people, but God through His Holy Spirit gave me to understand that this is what He wanted me to do, so I did."

We can do great things for God when we simply obey.

Truly, truly, I say to you, he who believes in Me,
the works that I do shall he do also; and greater works
than these shall he do; because I go to the Father.
John 14:12 NASB

Dost thou love life?

Then do not squander time, for that is the stuff life is made of.

A WOMAN once had a dream that an angel was giving her this message: "As a reward for your virtues, the sum of $1,440 will be deposited into your bank account every morning. This amount has only one condition. At the close of each business day, any balance that has not been used will be canceled. It won't carry over to the next day or accrue interest. Each morning, a new $1,440 will be credited to you."

The dream was so vivid, she asked the Lord to show her what it meant. He led her to realize she was receiving 1,440 minutes every morning, the total number of minutes in a twenty-four-hour day. What she did with this deposit of time was important, because 1,440 minutes per day was all she would ever receive!

Each of us has a similar account. What we do with those 1,440 minutes each day is up to us. At the close of each "business" day, we should be able to look over our ledger and see that these golden minutes were spent wisely.

Time is God's gift to you. What you do with your time is your gift to God.

Remember how short my time is.

Psalm 89:47

The grass may be greener on the other side, but it still has to be mowed.

SEVERAL years ago, a newspaper cartoon was drawn of two fields divided by a fence. Both were about the same size, and each had plenty of lush green grass.

Each field had a mule whose head stuck through the wire fence, eating grass from the other's pasture. Although each mule was surrounded by plenty of grass, the neighboring field seemed somewhat more desirable even though it was harder to reach.

In the process, the mules' heads became caught in the fence. They panicked and brayed uncontrollably at being unable to free themselves. The cartoonist wisely described the situation with one word: "DISCONTENT."

Like the mules, when we focus on what we don't have we become blinded to the blessings which surround us. There is nothing wrong with desiring something, but to think life is easier in someone else's pasture is folly. Besides, no matter where we are, we will always have to deal with the attitudes of our own heart.

If there is something you desire in life, perhaps a new home, a better car, or even your own business, look to Jesus to help you bring it to pass. Meanwhile, remember to find pleasure in what He's already given you!

Be content with such things as ye have.
Hebrews 13:5

Every job is a self-portrait of the person who does it. Autograph your work with excellence.

SOMEONE once asked Al Jolson, a popular musical comedy star of the twenties, what he did to warm up a cold audience. Jolson answered, "Whenever I go out before an audience and don't get the response I feel that I ought to get . . . I don't go back behind the scenes and say to myself, *That audience is dead from the neck up, it's a bunch of wooden nutmegs.* No, instead I say to myself, *Look here, Al, what is wrong with you tonight? The audience is all right, but you're all wrong, Al.*"

Many a performer has blamed a poor showing on an audience. Al Jolson took a different approach. He tried to give the best performance of his career to his coldest, most unresponsive audiences. The result was that before an evening was over he had them applauding and begging for more.

You'll always be able to find excuses for mediocrity. In fact, a person intent on justifying a bad performance usually has excuses lined up before the final curtain falls. Choose instead to put your full energy into everything you do. Your extra effort will turn an average performance into something outstanding.

The joys of a job well done—that is true satisfaction!

Many daughters have done well, But you excel them all.
Proverbs 31:29 NKJV

If a task is once begun, never leave it till it's done. Be the labor great or small, do it well or not at all.

86

A series of illustrations in a popular magazine once depicted the life story of a "one-note musician." From frame to frame, the tale revealed how the woman followed her daily routine until the time came for the evening concert. She carefully inspected her violin, took her seat among the other violinists, arranged her music on the stand, and tuned her instrument. As the concert began, the conductor skillfully cued first one group of musicians and then another until finally, the crucial moment arrived. It was time for the one note to be played!

The conductor turned to the violinist and signaled her to sound her note. She did, and then the moment was over. The orchestra played on while the "one-note" woman sat quietly through the rest of the concert—not with a sense of disappointment that she had played only one note, but with a sense of contentment and peace of mind that she had played her one note in tune, on time, and with great gusto.

Sometimes "one-note" people are criticized for being limited or narrow in their perspective by those whose lifestyle requires the playing of many notes. But a job well done is valued by God, whether it's one note or an entire symphony.

Whatever your hand finds to do, do it with your might.
Ecclesiastes 9:10 NKJV

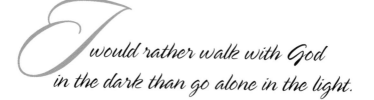

*I would rather walk with God
in the dark than go alone in the light.*

ON February 11, 1861, President-elect Lincoln left his home in Springfield to begin his rail journey to Washington, where he was to be inaugurated a month later. Lincoln had a premonition this would be the last time he would see Springfield. Standing on the rear platform of his railroad car, he bid the townspeople farewell. He closed his remarks with these words: "Today I leave you. I go to assume a task more difficult than that which devolved upon General Washington. The great God which guided him must help me. Without that assistance I shall surely fail; with it, I cannot fail."

The same is true for us, regardless of the tasks we face. Without God's assistance, we cannot succeed. We may get the dishes washed, the laundry folded, and the beds made—we may get our work done without accident or incident. We may find what we need at the market and manage to keep a schedule. But without God's help, our lives would be a confused mess.

Does God care about what happens in our day? Absolutely! When we become overwhelmed, He helps us to gather our thoughts. Step-by-step He shows us the way and our strength is renewed to go on.

Even when walking through the dark valley of death I will not be afraid, for you are close beside me, guarding, guiding all the way.

Psalm 23:4 TLB

*Remember
the banana—
when it left the bunch,
it got skinned.*

THE next time you visit a very dense forest, try to imagine what is taking place under your feet. Scientists now know when the roots of trees come into contact with one another, a substance which encourages the growth of a particular kind of fungus is released. This fungus helps link roots of different trees—even those of dissimilar species. If one tree has access to water, another to nutrients, and a third to sunlight, the fungus enables the transfer of these items to trees that may be in need. Thus the trees have the means of sharing with one another to preserve them all.

Our culture today applauds individualism. This isolates people from one another and cuts them off from the mainstream of life. With more and more people working at home or in walled offices, and with schedules crammed tighter than ever with work and activities, feelings of loneliness are more likely to increase than decrease. Don't allow isolation to overcome you!

Reach out to others. Begin to give where you can. Learn to receive when others give to you. Build a network of friends, not just colleagues. And above all, root yourself into a group that nourishes you spiritually—a church.

*Not forsaking the assembling of ourselves together,
as the manner of some is; but exhorting one another:
and so much the more, as ye see the day approaching.*
Hebrews 10:25

*D*ecisions can take you out
of *God's* will but never out of *His* reach.

WHEN Cathy met Jim at a softball game, she thought he was the perfect man for her. He was everything she was looking for! After several months of dating, Cathy was as sold on Jim as ever, except it bothered her that he found so many excuses for drinking alcohol. "I got a raise!" "My friend is getting married!" "My sister is graduating from college!"

Despite her friends' warnings and her own misgivings Cathy married Jim. Before long however, the marriage was destroyed by Jim's drinking. When the divorce was final, Cathy felt destroyed too. She had made one of the biggest mistakes a Christian could make. "I wanted to have my way instead of God's," Cathy told her pastor. "I thought I knew what was best for me."

"We all think that sometimes," Cathy's pastor said. "We forget that the One Who created us knows us better than we know ourselves. But remember, Cathy, He never gives up on us! When we admit our mistakes, He always forgives us and gives us another chance."

Recovering from the bad choices we've made can be heart-wrenching and difficult, but God is always right there, ready to make us whole and give us a brand-new life.

If we are faithless, he will remain faithful,
for he cannot disown himself.
2 Timothy 2:13 NIV

"*No*"

is one of

the few

94

words that

can never

be mis-

understood.

WHILE in medical training, surgeons are encouraged to weigh the importance of each word spoken during an operation. When anesthetic is given, fear may strike a patient if she hears someone say, "I'm going to shoot her now." Even a phrase such as "hook up the monitor" may be interpreted by a drugged patient as sounding like "shake up the monster." Can you imagine the impact on a half-dazed patient if she hears a doctor say, "This just isn't my day!"

Additionally, the same directions given by two different physicians could encourage or discourage a patient, simply by the tone of voice used. One doctor's voice might suggest a prescription will work, while another's might convey reservations. Either could drastically affect the morale of a patient.

Theodore Roosevelt popularized an expression about the need for clear, precise communication. He called words with several possible meanings "weasel words." By using them a speaker might weasel out of any commitment, claiming a different interpretation of the word.

The Bible also tells us again and again to remember the importance of our words. We should think carefully before we say whatever's on our mind. We are to always speak words of encouragement, hope, and faith to those around us.

But let your statement be, "Yes, yes" or "No, no."
Matthew 5:37 NASB

Some people complain because God put thorns on roses, while others praise Him for putting roses among thorns.

ONE rainy day a woman overheard someone say, "What miserable weather!" She looked out her office window to see a big fat robin using a nearby puddle of water for a bathtub. He was splashing and fluttering, thoroughly enjoying himself. She couldn't help but think, *Miserable for whom? It's all a matter of perspective.*

That's a lesson that Lincoln Steffens learned as a young boy. He was watching an artist paint a picture of a muddy river. He told the artist he didn't like the picture because there was so much mud in it. The artist admitted there was mud in the picture, but what he saw was the beautiful colors and contrasts of the light against the dark.

Steffens later preached in a sermon, "Mud or beauty, which do we look for as we journey through life? If we look for mud and ugliness, we find them—they are there. Just as the artist found beauty in the muddy river, because that is what he was looking for, we will find, in the stream of life, those things which we desire to see. To look for the best and see the beautiful is the way to get the best out of life each day."

Finally, brethren, whatsoever things are true, whatsoever things are honest, whatsoever things are just, whatsoever things are pure, whatsoever things are lovely, whatsoever things are of good report; if there be any virtue, and if there be any praise, think on these things.

Philippians 4:8

Real friends are those who, when you've made a fool of yourself, don't feel you've done a permanent job.

IN Brienne, Napoleon went to school with a young man named Demasis who greatly admired him. After Napoleon quelled the mob in Paris and served at Toulon, his authority was stripped from him and he became penniless. Therefore, with thoughts of suicide, he proceeded toward a bridge to throw himself into the waters below. On the way he met his old friend Demasis, who asked him what was troubling him.

Napoleon told him bluntly he was without money, and he despaired of his situation ever changing. "Oh, if that is all," Demasis said, "take this; it will supply your wants." He put a pouch of gold into his hands and walked away. Normally Napoleon would have never taken such a handout. But that night he did, and his hope was renewed.

When Napoleon came to power, he sought far and wide to thank and promote his friend, but he never found him. It was rumored that Demasis lived and served in one of Napoleon's own armies, but never revealed his true identity. He was content to serve quietly in support of the leader he admired.

Sometimes our simple words or deeds make all the difference in the world to someone who doesn't know where to turn.

[Love] bears all things, believes all things, hopes all things, endures all things. Love never fails.
1 Corinthians 13:7-8 NKJV

Conscience is God's built-in warning system. Be very happy when it hurts you. Be very worried when it doesn't.

100

KELLEY was surprised to find a hair dryer tucked into a corner of an old suitcase. For years she had used the case to store bits of fabric from her sewing projects. Now while piecing together a quilt, she had unearthed it. *Where did this come from?* she asked herself.

After several days of trying to remember, she finally recalled having used it while visiting friends nearly a decade before. She had made several visits to the family and had apparently placed the borrowed hair dryer into her case inadvertently. To complicate matters, the family had asked about its whereabouts, and she had replied that she didn't have a clue!

Embarrassed, she thought, *How can I tell my friends after all these years that I have this?* However, her conscience wouldn't let the matter rest. She finally sent the hair dryer back to the family with an apology and an explanation. With many laughs, all was quickly forgiven.

When we ignore our conscience, it becomes callused and no longer sensitive. A healthy conscience is one of our greatest gifts from God. It serves to keep our lives on track and thus maintain peace in our hearts.

And herein do I exercise myself, to have always
a conscience void of offence toward God, and toward men.
Acts 24:16

*you don't stand for
something you'll fall
for anything!*

A saleswoman passed a particular corner each day on her way to work. One day, she observed a young girl trying to sell a floppy-eared puppy. After a week, the saleswoman finally said to the girl, "Honey, if you really want to sell this dog, then I suggest you clean him up and make people think they're getting something big." At noon, the saleswoman noticed the girl had taken her advice. The puppy was groomed and sitting under a big sign: "TREEMENNDOUS Puppy for Sale $5,000."

To her surprise, on the way home she saw the puppy was gone! Flabbergasted, the woman sought out the girl to ask if she had really sold the dog for $5,000.

The girl replied, "I sure did, and I want to thank you for all your help." The saleswoman stuttered, "How in the world did you do it?" The girl said, "It was easy. I just took two $2,500 cats in exchange!"

Two thousand years ago there was another great exchange. Jesus Christ gave His life in exchange for ours. What value did He see in us? We were His prized creation, stolen for a season by our own will, but now repurchased as His beloved possession.

For ye are bought with a price: therefore glorify God in your body, and in your spirit, which are God's.
1 Corinthians 6:20

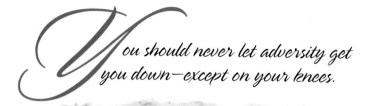

You should never let adversity get you down—except on your knees.

GOD'S LITTLE DEVOTIONAL BOOK FOR WOMEN

MANY people see abundant spring rains as a great blessing to farmers, especially if the rains come after the plants have sprouted and are several inches tall. However, what they don't realize is even a short drought can have a devastating effect on a crop of seedlings that have received too much rain.

Why? Because during frequent rains, the young plants are not required to push their roots deeper into the soil in search of water. If a drought occurs later, plants with shallow root systems will quickly die.

We often receive abundance into our lives—rich fellowship, great teaching, thorough soakings of spiritual blessings. Yet when stress or tragedy enters our lives, we may find ourselves thinking God has abandoned us or is unfaithful. The fact is, we have allowed the ease of our lives to keep us from pushing our spiritual roots deeper. We have allowed others to spoon-feed us, rather than develop our own deep personal relationship with God through prayer and study of His Word.

Only the deeply rooted are able to endure hard times without wilting. The best advice is to enjoy the rain while seeking to grow even closer to Him.

For I am persuaded, that neither death, nor life,
nor angels, nor principalities, nor powers, nor things present,
nor things to come . . . shall be able to separate us from
the love of God, which is in Christ Jesus our Lord.
Romans 8:38-39

*The best bridge between hope and despair
is often a good night's sleep.*

MEDICAL researchers have recently come to what may seem a common-sense conclusion: a missing ingredient to health may be "vitamin Zzzzzzzz."

When participants in one study were cheated out of four hours of sleep for four consecutive nights, they had on average a 30 percent drop in their immune systems, as measured by natural killer-cell activity. Such a drop can readily increase a person's susceptibility to colds and flu, and perhaps to other serious diseases. Says sleep researcher Michael Irwin, M.D., "Many people just need a regular-length sleep to get those natural killer cells revved up again.

"While a steady diet of sufficient sleep may not completely prevent disease, it can improve the body's defense system and help a person combat disease more efficiently and effectively."

Sleep is the cheapest health aid a person can use. Sleep is our God-given means of restoring health to the body, as well as providing rest to the mind. People often report a new outlook or a change of heart after a good night's sleep.

Ask God to renew your strength as you sleep tonight; then get to bed on time, so He can give you what you requested!

It is vain for you to rise up early, to sit up late, to eat the bread of sorrows: for so he giveth his beloved sleep.
Psalm 127:2

*It's good to be a Christian and know it,
but it's better to be a Christian and show it!*

BEFORE the colonialists imposed national boundaries, the kings of Laos and Vietnam had already reached an agreement about who was Laotian and who was Vietnamese. Those who ate short-grain rice, built their houses on stilts, and decorated their homes with Indian-style serpents were considered Laotians. Those who ate long-grain rice, built their houses on the ground, and decorated their homes with Chinese-style dragons were Vietnamese. The kings taxed the people accordingly and had little use for boundaries apart from this designation.

The kings knew it was not the exact location of a person's home that determined their culture or loyalty. Instead, each person belonged to the kingdom whose values they shared.

We can often identify a person's nationality by their tastes in food, clothing, and art. Their lifestyle is evidence of their cultural influences.

So it is with a Christian. Regardless of our culture or nationality, we belong to God's kingdom. We live according to the values, standards, and commandments He has established. When we pray, "Thy kingdom come, Thy will be done," we are asking that the heavenly law of love become established in our lives here on earth. We are His people, regardless of our address.

By this shall all men know that ye are my disciples,
if ye have love one to another.
John 13:35

Sometimes we are so busy adding up our troubles that we forget to count our blessings.

IN some parts of Mexico, hot springs and cold springs are found side by side. Because of this natural phenomenon, local women have the convenience of boiling their clothes in the hot springs, then rinsing them in the adjacent cold springs. While watching this procedure a number of years ago, a tourist said to her guide, "I imagine that they think old Mother Nature is pretty generous to supply such ample, clean hot and cold water here side by side for their free use."

The guide replied, "Well, actually, no. There is much grumbling because Mother Nature supplies no soap! And not only that, but the rumor has started to filter in that there are machines that do this work in other parts of the world."

So often we compare our lives to others'—what they have in contrast to what we don't have, and what they are that we aren't. Such comparisons invariably leave us feeling left out, rejected, and cheated. If we aren't careful to put the brakes on such negative emotions, we can become unnecessarily bitter.

Gratitude can go a long way in changing your attitude. Count your blessings today! If you own one, start with—a washing machine.

I will remember the works of the LORD:
surely I will remember thy wonders of old.
I will meditate also of all thy work, and talk of thy doings.
Psalm 77:11-12

*Be
more concerned
with what
God thinks
about you than
what people think
about you.*

A pastor's wife was intrigued when she heard a person say, "One hour is only 4 percent of a day." She had not thought about time in this way. Desiring more prayer time in her life, she thought surely she could give God at least 4 percent of her day. She determined to try it.

Therefore, rather than try to fit prayer into her schedule, she decided to fix a prayer time, and then fit the rest of the day around it. Her children were now old enough to travel to school alone, so by 8:30 each morning, a hush fell over her home. She knew her best hour for prayer would be between 8:30 and 9:30 A.M. To guarantee she was uninterrupted, she made it known in the parish that, except for emergencies, she would be grateful if people didn't call her until after 9:30 in the morning.

To her surprise, no one in the church was offended. Instead they responded very positively. Several other women began to follow her example by setting aside the same hour to pray every day!

When we seek God's plan first, our plans with other people will have a way of falling into place.

But seek first the kingdom of God and His righteousness, and all these things shall be added to you.
Matthew 6:33 NKJV

The best way to get the last word is to apologize.

IN 1755, a twenty-three-year-old colonel was in the midst of running for a seat in the Virginia assembly when he made an insulting remark about an opponent, as part of a campaign speech. The remark was addressed to a hot-tempered man named Payne, who responded by knocking the colonel down with a hickory stick. Soldiers rushed to the colonel's aid, and it appeared that a full-blown fight would ensue. But the would-be politician got up, dusted himself off, called off the soldiers, and left the scene.

The next morning the colonel wrote Payne a note requesting his presence at a local tavern. Payne obliged, but wondered what motives and demands the colonel might make. To Payne's surprise, the colonel met him with an apology, asking forgiveness for his derogatory remarks and offering a handshake.

The move may have been viewed by others as politically expedient. However, Colonel George Washington considered it personally imperative, if he was to enjoy internal peace as he continued with his campaign.

Our human sense of justice would have demanded that Payne be the one to apologize, but Colonel Washington chose to extend mercy. The moment we feel like demanding forgiveness from others may be the moment when we are to forgive.

If you have been trapped by what you said, ensnared by the words of your mouth . . . Go and humble yourself; press your plea with your neighbor!
Proverbs 6:2-3 NIV

Forget yourself for others and others will not forget you!

116

MILLIE was a mentally retarded adult who lived with her mother in a small town. She was well-known for her proverbial "green thumb." Lawns, hedges, and flower beds flourished under her loving attention. Millie also volunteered by cutting grass and weeds, raking leaves, and planting flowers in vacant lots throughout the town. Her trademark was her oil can. She always carried a small can of lubricating oil in her hip pocket and applied a dose of oil to any squeaky door, hinge, or gate she encountered.

On Sundays Millie went to church with her mother. When she was teased, she refused to respond in any way other than with good humor and unflappable cheer.

When Millie died, everyone in town showed up for her funeral. There were scores of people who traveled from distant places to attend, including many of those who had once teased her.

Without consciously attempting to do so, Millie exemplified good citizenship. She worked hard, remained optimistic, eased tensions, and faithfully attended church.

We may sometimes be tempted to quit doing the little things, thinking no one will miss it. However, Millie's life shows us that others really do notice the small things we do for them in love and kindness.

Therefore all things whatsoever ye would that men should do to you, do ye even so to them: for this is the law and the prophets.
Matthew 7:12

Those who bring sunshine to the lives of others cannot keep it from themselves.

THERE was a wealthy noblewoman who had grown tired of life. She had everything one could wish for, except happiness and contentment. She said, "I am weary of life. I will go to the river and there end my life."

As she walked toward the river, she suddenly felt a little hand tugging at her skirts. Looking down, she saw a frail little boy who pleaded, "There are six of us. We are dying for want of food!" The noblewoman thought, *Why should I not relieve this wretched family? I have the means, and it seems I will have no more use for riches when I am gone.*

Following the little boy, she entered a scene of great want. She opened her purse and emptied its contents. The family members were beside themselves with joy and gratitude. The noblewoman said, "I'll return tomorrow, and I will share with you more of the good things which God has given to me in abundance!

She left rejoicing that the child had found her. For the first time in her life she understood the reason for her wealth. Never again did she think of ending her life, which was now filled with meaning and a purpose—giving.

119

Be not deceived; God is not mocked: for
whatsoever a man soweth, that shall he also reap.
Galatians 6:7

God plus one is always a majority!

CARDINAL von Faulhaber of Munich is reported once to have had a conversation with the famed physicist, Albert Einstein.

"Cardinal von Faulhaber," Einstein said, "I respect religion, but I believe in mathematics. Probably it is the other way around with you."

"You are mistaken," replied the Cardinal. "To me, both are merely different expressions of the same divine exactness."

"But, your Eminence, what would you say if mathematical science should someday come to conclusions directly contradictory to religious beliefs?"

"Oh," the Cardinal answered with ease, "I have the highest respect for the competence of mathematicians. I am sure they would never rest until they discovered their mistake."

Regardless of how ardently some people try to suppress it, God's truth will always prevail! You can be confident, the Maker of the heavens and the earth will make His truth known. Even in the smallest details of your life, He will reveal His truth to you in order to lead you on the right path. God will never leave you or forsake you. You can overcome any obstacle, knowing that the God Who set the planets in their orbits also knit you together in your mother's womb and placed His Spirit within you. He is with you always.

If God be for us, who can be against us?
Romans 8:31

Jesus is a friend who knows all your faults and still loves you anyway.

AT a crucial time in her life, a young Christian woman cried out to the Lord. She was despairing over the lack of spiritual power and fruitfulness she was experiencing in her walk with God. Suddenly she sensed Jesus standing beside her, asking, "May I have the keys to your life?"

The experience was so realistic, the woman reached into her pocket and took out a ring of keys.

"Are all the keys here?" the Lord asked.

"Yes, except the key to one small room in my life."

"If you cannot trust Me in all rooms of your life, I cannot accept any of the keys."

The woman was so overwhelmed at the thought of the Lord moving out of her life altogether, she cried, "Lord! Take the keys to all the rooms of my life."

Many of us have rooms we hope no one will ever see. We intend to clean them out someday, but someday never seems to come. When we invite Jesus into these rooms, He will help us clean them. With Him, we will have the courage to throw away all the junk, and He will fill the rooms with His love and peace and joy.

*But God commendeth his love toward us, in that,
while we were yet sinners, Christ died for us.*
Romans 5:8

*Every person should have a special
cemetery lot in which to bury the faults
of friends and loved ones.*

THE Bible tells us that God removes our sins as far as the east is from the west. (Psalm 103:12.) Our sins are forgotten by God, so we should forget them too. The following story beautifully illustrates that point:

A much-loved minister of God once carried a secret burden of long-past sin buried deep in his heart. He had committed the sin many years before, during his seminary training. No one knew what he had done, but they did know he had repented. Even so, he had suffered years of remorse over the incident, without any sense of God's forgiveness.

A woman in his church deeply loved God and claimed to have visions in which Jesus Christ spoke to her. The minister, skeptical of her claims, asked of her, "The next time you speak to the Lord, would you please ask Him what sin your minister committed while he was in seminary?" The woman agreed to ask.

When she came to the church a few days later the minister asked, "Did He visit you?"

She said, "Yes."

"And did you ask Him what sin I committed in seminary?"

"Yes, I asked Him," she replied.

"Well, what did He say?"

"He said, 'I don't remember.'"

And be ye kind one to another, tenderhearted, forgiving one another, even as God for Christ's sake hath forgiven you.

Ephesians 4:32

A minute of thought is worth
more than an hour of talk.

126

A heart doctor was amazed at the great improvement one of his patients had made. When he had seen the woman in the hospital a few months earlier, she was seriously ill. He asked the woman what had happened.

The woman said, "I was sure the end was near and that you and your staff had given up hope. However, Thursday morning something happened that changed everything. You listened to my heart; and you announced to all those standing about my bed that I had a 'wholesome gallop.' I knew that the doctors might try to soften things in talking to me, but I knew they wouldn't kid each other. So when I overheard you tell your colleagues I had a 'wholesome gallop,' I figured I still had a lot of kick to my heart and could not be dying. My spirits were for the first time lifted, and I knew I would live and recover."

The heart doctor never told the woman that a "gallop" is a poor sign that denotes the heart muscle is straining and usually failing!

Just a few words can be enough to make a difference in a person's life. How important it is to choose our words wisely.

Set a watch, O LORD, before my mouth; keep the door of my lips.
❦ Psalm 141:3 ❧

*You can win
more friends
with your ears
than with your
mouth.*

DALE Carnegie, author of *How To Win Friends and Influence People*, is considered one of the greatest "friend winners" of the century. He taught, "You can make more friends in two months by becoming interested in other people than you can in two years by trying to get other people interested in you."

To illustrate his point, Carnegie would tell how dogs have learned the fine art of making friends better than most people. When you get within ten feet of a friendly dog, he will begin to wag his tail, a visible sign that he welcomes and enjoys your presence. If you take time to pet the dog, he will become excited, lick you, and jump all over you to show how much he appreciates you. The dog became man's best friend by being genuinely interested in people!

One of the foremost ways, of course, in which we show our interest in others is to listen to them and ask questions, intently listen to their answers, and to ask further questions. The person who feels heard is likely to seek out his friendly listener again and again, and to count that person as a great friend.

Need a friend? Start listening.

Let every man be swift to hear, slow to speak, slow to wrath.
James 1:19

*It's not the
outlook but the
uplook that
counts.*

THE story of Helen Keller is well-known. Deaf and blind from a childhood disease, the world was opened up to Helen through her teacher, Anne Sullivan. She taught Helen to rely on her other senses of taste, touch, and smell to experience life. In her autobiography, Helen Keller wrote:

"Fate silent, pitiless bars the way. Fain would I question his imperious decree; for my heart is undisciplined and passionate, but my tongue will not utter the bitter, futile words that rise to my lips, and they fall back into my heart like unshed tears. Silence sits immense upon my soul. Then comes hope with a smile and whispers, *There is joy in self-forgetfulness.* So I try to make the light in other people's eyes my sun, the music in others' ears my symphony, the smile on others' lips my happiness."

How sad it is when we search only within ourselves for a reason to be happy, because the happiness in those around us is reason enough to give us joy, regardless of our situation or handicap. And if the poor and the handicapped can have joy, how can we wallow in depression?

If we look to Jesus, all will be well with us—inside and out.

Looking unto Jesus the author and finisher of our faith.
Hebrews 12:2

It isn't hard to make a mountain out of a molehill. Just add a little dirt.

132

SUSAN was deeply disappointed at the lack of emotional intimacy she felt in her marriage, and she began to lash out at her husband. He, of course, reacted with his own defensive anger. Over time their anger grew, heated words were exchanged, and eventually threats of divorce became part of their confrontations. Finally, Susan's husband moved out and she filed for divorce.

The divorce proceedings were bitter. They fought through the entire process. When they met to sign the final papers, they stopped to look at each other and Susan saw in her husband's eyes the very feelings she was experiencing—a feeling of longing and yet of resignation. She thought, *I don't want to divorce him, and I don't think he wants to divorce me.*

She voiced her thoughts to her husband, and for a moment it appeared he might also soften and admit he too still cared. But then he said in a dull monotone, "We've come this far, I guess we should finish it." Susan left the courtroom realizing she had never really wanted a divorce. She had just wanted her husband to listen.

Don't allow anger to lead you anywhere—especially down a road you truly don't want to travel.

Starting a quarrel is like breaching a dam;
so drop the matter before a dispute breaks out.
Proverbs 17:14 NIV

Jesus is a friend who walks in when the world has walked out.

134

WHILE serving in India, a devout English judge befriended a young Indian man. He had been raised in a prominent Indian family but had been cast out after he converted to Christianity. The judge took the boy into his household where the boy happily worked as a servant.

It was the custom of the household to have a devotional time every evening. One night the judge read aloud the words of Jesus: "Every one that hath forsaken houses, or brethren, or sisters, or father, or mother, or wife, or children, or lands, for my name's sake, shall receive an hundredfold." (Matthew 19:29.)

The judge turned to the lad and said, "Nobody here has done this except you, Norbudur. Will you tell us, is it true what Jesus has said?"

The young Indian man read the verse aloud for himself and then turned to the family and said, "No, there is an error."

Startled, the judge responded, "There is?"

The youth replied, "It says He gives a hundredfold. I know He gives a thousandfold."

Eternal life, intimacy with the Father, and all the riches of heaven—how can we truly measure the value of what it means when Jesus Christ comes into a person's life?

In the world ye shall have tribulation: but be of good cheer;
I have overcome the world.
John 16:33

A critical spirit is like poison ivy—it only takes a little contact to spread its poison.

A little girl once asked her father how wars got started.

"Well," said her father, "suppose America persisted in quarreling with England, and. . . ."

"But," interrupted her mother, "America must never quarrel with England."

"I know," said the father, "but I am only using a hypothetical instance."

"But you are misleading the child," protested Mom.

"No, I am not," replied the father indignantly, with an edge of anger in his voice.

"Never mind, Daddy," the little girl interjected. "I think I know how wars get started."

Most major arguments don't begin large but are rooted in small annoyances. It's like the mighty oak that stood on the skyline of the Rocky Mountains. The tree had survived hail, heavy snows, bitter cold, and ferocious storms for more than a century. It was finally felled not by a great lightning strike or an avalanche, but by an attack of tiny beetles.

A little hurt, neglect, or insult can be the beginning of the end for virtually any relationship. One careless word can start a wound that grows with each additional comment. Little by little, it can eventually inflict great pain. Therefore, take care what you say and be certain that you're speaking in love.

But avoid worldly and empty chatter,
for it will lead to further ungodliness.
2 Timothy 2:16 NASB

*K*indness is the oil that takes
the friction out of life.

A number of years ago, the Advertising and Sales Executive Club sponsored a Courtesy Campaign in Kansas City, Kansas. One thousand silver dollars were flown in from Denver. Then, over a period of days, "mystery shoppers" visited all types of stores, banks, and other places of business. They listened to telephone operators and observed bus and street-car drivers. Each day they filed a written report on the persons they found to be the most courteous.

Those chosen as the most courteous people in the city received a silver dollar, along with a "courtesy pays" button and a congratulatory card. The fifteen most outstandingly courteous people were guests at a banquet, where they were awarded $25 each. In all, more than 100 people were honored.

What resulted was not only a temporary increase in the courtesy of the local residents, but an awareness throughout the city that simple kindness is a nice thing with which to live! This residual effect remained long after the campaign. Today, Kansas City is still regarded as one of the friendliest cities in the nation.

It doesn't cost anything to be kind, but kindness can pay off in big ways much more meaningful than money!

But the fruit of the Spirit is . . . kindness.
Galatians 5:22 NIV

*Our days are identical suitcases—
all the same size but some people
can pack more into them than others.*

MARY Smith went to church one Sunday morning and winced when she heard the organist miss a note during the processional. She was irritated by a teenager talking while everyone was supposed to be praying. She also couldn't help but notice that several blooms in the altar bouquets were wilted. She felt the usher was scrutinizing what every person was putting into the offering plate, which made her angry. And she counted at least five grammatical errors in the preacher's sermon. After the closing hymn, as she left the church through the side door, she thought, *What a careless group of people!*

Amy Jones went to church one Sunday morning and was thrilled by the choir's rendition of "A Mighty Fortress." Her heart was touched at hearing a teenager read the morning Scripture lesson. She was encouraged to see the church taking up an offering to help hungry children in Nigeria. The preacher's sermon answered a question that had bothered her for some time. And she felt radiant joy from the choir members during the recessional. She left the church thinking, *What a wonderful place to worship God!*

Mary and Amy went to the same church, on the same Sunday morning.

Be very careful, then, how you live—not as unwise but as wise, making the most of every opportunity.
Ephesians 5:15-16 NIV

To forgive is to set a prisoner free and discover the prisoner was you.

MEREDITH was surprised to find a letter in her mailbox from her brother, Tim. It had been three years since she had spoken to him, even though they lived in the same town. In the letter, Tim told her he and his wife were expecting twins and he hoped she would come to visit the babies after they were born. He expressed his sorrow that they had not communicated more, and apologized for whatever it was he had done to cause them to become estranged.

Meredith's initial reaction was anger. "Whatever it was?" *Didn't he know?* She immediately sat down and wrote a five-page letter detailing all the things Tim had done to hurt her. The phone rang before she could put her letter in an envelope, however, and it was several hours before she returned to her writing desk. Upon rereading her letter, she was horrified at what she found.

She had thought she was being very matter of fact, but her words were full of anger and pain. Tears of forgiveness filled her eyes. *Perhaps it wasn't all Tim's fault.*

She called him the next day to say, "I can hardly wait to be the aunt of twins!"

For if ye forgive men their trespasses, your heavenly Father will also forgive you: But if ye forgive not men their trespasses, neither will your Father forgive your trespasses.
Matthew 6:14-15

The heart is the happiest
when it beats for others.

144

ALBERT Einstein once reflected on the purpose of man's existence: "Strange is our situation here upon earth. Each of us comes for a short visit, not knowing why, yet sometimes seeming to a divine purpose. From the standpoint of daily life, however, there is one thing we do know: That we are here for the sake of others . . . for the countless unknown souls with whose fate we are connected by a bond of sympathy. Many times a day, I realize how much my own outer and inner life is built upon the labors of people, both living and dead, and how earnestly I must exert myself in order to give in return as much as I have received."

When we truly take stock of our lives, we must admit we have done nothing on our own. Our thinking has been fashioned by our many teachers and mentors, including family members. Our ability to function physically is the result, in part, of our genetic code and the productivity of others in providing food, water, and shelter. Our spiritual lives are a gift of God Himself.

We are what we have received. These facts should drive us to share our lives with others.

Greater love hath no man than this,
that a man lay down his life for his friends.
John 15:13

God has a history of using the insignificant to accomplish the impossible.

IN order to communicate among themselves, Serbian shepherd boys developed an ingenious system. They would stick the blades of their long knives into the ground of a pasture, and when one of the boys sensed an approaching cattle thief, he would strike the handle of his knife sharply. The vibration created a signal that could be picked up by other shepherd boys who had their ears pressed tightly against the ground. It was by this unique system that they outwitted thieves who tried to creep up on their flocks and herds under the cover of darkness and tall corn.

Most of the shepherd boys grew up and forgot about their ground signals, but one boy remembered. Twenty-five years after he left the pastures, he made one of the greatest inventions of the modern era. Michael Pupin changed the telephone from a device used only to speak across a city, to a long-distance instrument that could be heard across a continent.

Something you take for granted today, something others may consider to be insignificant or ordinary, may actually become your key to greatness. Look around you. What is it that God has put at your disposal? Ask Him to open your eyes to the possibilities.

And Jesus looking upon them saith, With men it is impossible, but not with God: for with God all things are possible.
Mark 10:27

I make it a rule of Christian duty never to go to a place where there is not room for my Master as well as myself.

AN attractive single woman had a job that required a great deal of travel. When a new female colleague was added to her department, she told her how happy she was to have another woman on the team. She related how she often felt isolated when she found herself the only woman at breakfast in a hotel restaurant, or one of only a handful of women on a commuter flight.

"Do the men ever bother you?" the young new colleague asked.

"Rarely," the woman replied.

"Wow," said the young colleague. "You are so beautiful, I would think you are approached a great deal by men you really don't care to meet."

"Oh, I am approached," the woman explained, "but I just say five words and immediately I am left alone."

"Five words?" the young colleague asked, hoping to gain a valuable tip. "What are they?"

"When I am approached by a man," the woman said, "I simply ask, 'Are you a born-again Christian?'"

"Has anyone ever said 'yes'?" the younger asked.

"Rarely," said the woman. "And when such men want to talk to me anyway, I always have an enjoyable conversation, because Jesus can be part of it."

That's just one of the benefits of taking Jesus everywhere you go!

Don't be teamed with those who do not love the Lord. . . .
How can a Christian be a partner with one who doesn't believe?
2 Corinthians 6:14–15 TLB

Jesus can turn water into wine, but He can't turn your whining into anything.

RATHER than whining that we don't have certain things in our lives or that something is wrong, we need to take positive action. Here are four steps toward turning whining into thanksgiving.

1. *Give something away.* When you give something, you create both a physical and a mental space for something new and better to come into your life. Although you may think you are "lacking" something in life, when you give you demonstrate you have abundance to spare.

2. *Narrow your goals.* Don't expect everything good to come into your life all at once. When you focus your expectations toward specific and reachable goals, you are more apt to direct your time and energy toward reaching them.

3. *Change your vocabulary from "I need" to "I want."* Most of the things we think we need are actually things we want. When we receive them, we are more likely to be thankful for them as luxuries rather than necessities.

4. *Choose to be thankful for what you already have.* Thanksgiving is a choice we make. Every one of us has more things to be thankful for than we could begin to recount in a day, but we can always try!

Do all things without murmurings and disputings.
Philippians 2:14

The smallest deed is better than the greatest intention!

152

A MISSIONARY was sailing home when she was awakened by a cry—a cry that is perhaps the most difficult to hear when at sea: "Man overboard!" She arose quickly from her berth, lit the lamp on the bracket in her cabin, and then held the lamp at the window of her cabin in hopes of seeing some sign of life in the murky dark waters outside.

Seeing nothing, she hung the lamp back on its bracket, snuffed it out, and returned to her berth with prayers for the man lost at sea. In the morning, to her surprise she discovered the man had been rescued. Not only that, but she learned it was the flash of her lamp through the porthole that showed those on deck the location of the missing man, who was desperately clinging to a rope still attached to the deck. He was pulled from the cold waters in the nick of time. Such a small deed as shining a lamp at the right time had saved a man's life.

It isn't the size of the deed you do that counts. God can take *every* deed we perform and use it for His purposes, in our lives and in the lives of others.

Let us not love [merely] in theory or in speech but in deed and in truth (in practice and in sincerity).

1 John 3:18 AMP

I've suffered a great many catastrophes in my life. Most of them never happened.

A MILITARY chaplain, who was curious about how sensible it was to worry, once drew up a "Worry Table" based upon the problems men and women had brought to him through his years of service. He found their worries fit into these categories:

Worries about things that never happened, 40 percent

Worries about past, unchangeable decisions, 30 percent

Worries about illness that never happened, 12 percent

Worries about adult children and friends (who were able to take care of themselves), 10 percent

Worries about real problems, 8 percent

According to his chart, 52 percent of all worries are about things we can't control, concerns which are better left to God. And 40 percent are things that never happen, whether they are things we can control or not. The truth is, most of our anxieties are rooted in a failure to trust God. We simply don't believe He is big enough or cares enough to handle our problems, give us the desires of our hearts, or keep us and our loved ones from harm.

One of the most effective things we can do to combat worry is to spend time in God's Word, learning Who He is. Knowing God's character, we can easily see how we worry for nothing most of the time!

For God hath not given us the spirit of fear; but of power, and of love, and of a sound mind.

2 Timothy 1:7

If you want to make an easy job seem mighty hard, just keep putting off doing it.

WHEN Beth's boss asked her to take on an extra project, Beth saw the opportunity to prove she could handle greater responsibility. She immediately began to think how she might approach the task, and her enthusiasm ran high. But when the time came to actually start the project, Beth found herself telling her boss she was too busy to do the job justice. The project was given to someone else, who earned a promotion for completing it successfully. Beth didn't receive any new opportunities and eventually took a position with another firm.

What had kept Beth from doing the project? Simple procrastination. She put off getting started on the job until she was paralyzed with fear—fear that she might not be able to do the job or that her performance would not meet her boss' expectations. In the end, Beth didn't move ahead and thus reinforced her fears with a bigger sense of insecurity about her own ability.

If you find yourself procrastinating, ask God to show you how to overcome your fear; then do what He says. He wants you to succeed and live a fulfilled life. When you step out in faith, God will bless you!

How long are ye slack to go to possess the land,
which the LORD God of your fathers hath given you?
Joshua 18:3

Love sees through a telescope, not a microscope.

GOD'S LITTLE DEVOTIONAL BOOK FOR WOMEN

ON Christmas morning, little Amy was delighted to find a beautiful golden-haired doll among the presents she unwrapped. "She's so pretty!" Amy squealed in excitement as she hugged her new doll. Then rushing to hug her grandmother, the giver of the doll, she cried, "Thank you, thank you, thank you!"

Amy played with her new doll most of the day, but toward evening she put it down and sought out one of her old dolls. Amy cradled the tattered and dilapidated old doll in her arms. Its hair had nearly worn away, its nose was broken, one eye was askew, and an arm was missing.

"Well, well," Grandma noted, "it seems as though you like that old dolly better."

"I like the beautiful doll you gave me, Grandma," little Amy explained, "but I love this old doll more, because if I didn't love her, no one else would."

We all know the saying, "Beauty is in the eye of the beholder." A similar saying might be, "Love is the choice of the beholder." When we see faults in others, we can choose to look beyond them. We can choose to love them regardless of their negative attributes, faults, or quirks. After all, that's how God loves us.

Love endures long and is patient and kind . . . it takes no account of the evil done to it [it pays no attention to a suffered wrong].
1 Corinthians 13:4-5 AMP

A pint of example is worth a barrelful of advice.

EACH year on the fourth Sunday of July, the descendants of Roberto and Raquel Beaumont celebrate "Offspring Day." They have been doing this since 1956, when Raquel gathered her five preteen children around the dinner table. She placed a rose by the napkin of each daughter and a carnation by the napkin of each son.

Knowing in a few years her children would be going their separate ways, she told her children that the gifts she gave to them on Offspring Day were not mere flowers, but a token of her true gifts to them—time and love. Furthermore, she expected them to pass on those same gifts to their own children. Through the years, Raquel was the best example of her message: she always had time and love for each of her children, who regularly sought her advice and encouragement.

On Offspring Day each year, the elders who gather offer words of wisdom to their children. The young are encouraged to pick one thing about themselves they hope to improve in the coming year. It is a time for the generations to hear from one another and to set new goals for relationships.

With God's help, you can leave your children the lasting legacy of a good example.

Brethren, join in following my example, and observe those
who walk according to the pattern you have in us.
Philippians 3:17 NASB

If you were given a nickname descriptive of your character, would you be proud of it?

IN 1955 the city buses in Montgomery, Alabama, were segregated by law. White people and black people were not allowed to sit together.

On December 1 of that year, Mrs. Rosa Parks was riding the bus home from her job at a tailor shop. As the section for whites filled up, the black people were ordered to move to the back to make room for the white passengers who were boarding. Three blacks in Mrs. Parks' row moved, but Mrs. Parks remained in her seat. Later she said, "Our mistreatment was just not right, and I was tired of it. I knew someone had to take the first step. So I made up my mind not to move."

The bus driver asked her if she was going to stand up. "No, I am not," she answered. Mrs. Parks was arrested and taken to jail. Four days later black people and white sympathizers organized a boycott of the city bus line that lasted until a year later, when the Supreme Court declared the segregated-bus ordinance unconstitutional.

Mrs. Parks is known today as the "mother of the modern-day civil rights movement." Her name inspires others to be courageous and do what is right, despite the consequences.

A good name is rather to be chosen than great riches.
Proverbs 22:1

Tact is the art of making a point without making an enemy.

IN looking over a cafe menu, a woman noticed that both a chicken salad sandwich and a chicken sandwich were listed. She decided to order the chicken salad sandwich, but absentmindedly wrote "chicken sandwich" on her order slip. When the waiter brought the chicken sandwich, she protested immediately, insisting the waiter had erred.

Most waiters would have picked up the order slip and shown the customer their mistake. But instead, this waiter expressed his regret at the error, picked up the sandwich, returned to the kitchen, and a moment later placed a chicken salad sandwich in front of the woman.

While eating her sandwich, the woman picked up her order slip and noticed the mistake she had made. When it was time to pay for the meal, she apologized to the waiter and offered to pay for both sandwiches. The waiter said, "No, ma'am. That's perfectly all right. I'm just happy you've forgiven me for being right."

The truth always has a way of coming out eventually. We often just make a situation worse by defending ourselves. And we may say something we will later regret. It's best to respond to others with love and patience, believing that God will reveal the truth at the right moment.

Reckless words pierce like a sword,
but the tongue of the wise brings healing.
Proverbs 12:18 NIV

The best antique is an old friend.

A WOMAN was in a serious automobile accident in a city far from home. She felt so enclosed in a cocoon of pain, she didn't realize how lonely she was until an old friend in the city came to visit her. She firmly but gently said to her, "You should not be alone."

In the weeks that followed, this friend's advice rang in the injured woman's ears and helped her to overcome her otherwise reserved nature. When another friend called from a city several hundred miles away to say she wanted to come stay with her, the injured woman didn't say, "Don't bother" as would have been her normal response. Rather, she said, "Please come." The friend was a wonderful encouragement to her, reading the Psalms aloud when she was still too weak to read herself. Then yet another friend offered to come and help in her recovery. Again she swallowed her pride and said, "Please do."

Even Jesus did not carry His own cross all the way to Calvary. Another helped Him to shoulder His burden. It's all right to ask for help and to receive help when you haven't asked. You don't have to go it alone. Let a friend help you!

Your own friend and your father's friend, forsake them not. . . . Better is a neighbor who is near [in spirit] than a brother who is far off [in heart].

Proverbs 27:10 AMP

If you can't feed a hundred people then just feed one.

WHEN thirteen-year-old Bobby Hill, the son of a U.S. Army sergeant stationed in Italy, read a book about the work of Nobel Prize winner Albert Schweitzer, he decided to do something to help the medical missionary. He sent a bottle of aspirin to Lieutenant General Richard C. Lindsay, Commander of the Allied air forces in Southern Europe, asking if any of his airplanes could parachute the bottle of aspirin to Dr. Schweitzer's jungle hospital in Africa.

Upon hearing about the letter, an Italian radio station issued an appeal, resulting in more than $400,000 worth of donated medical supplies. The French and Italian governments each supplied a plane to fly the medicines and the boy to Dr. Schweitzer. The grateful doctor responded "I never thought a child could do so much for my hospital."

No one can solve all the problems in the world, but we can feed the hungry family in a nearby neighborhood, clothe the homeless person who has just arrived at a shelter, or give a blanket to the street person who lives near our office building. If every person who could help would determine to meet just one person's need every month, think what might be accomplished! One small gesture can multiply many times.

As we have therefore opportunity, let us do good unto all men.
Galatians 6:10

The trouble with stretching the truth is that it's apt to snap back.

A SUNDAY school teacher once told her adult class, "Next Sunday I am going to teach a very important lesson. I want you all to read chapter seventeen of St. Mark's Gospel in preparation for it." The members of the class nodded, indicating a willingness to do as the teacher requested.

The following Sunday the teacher asked the class, "Those who read chapter seventeen of St. Mark's Gospel during this past week, please raise your hands." Nearly all the people in the room raised their hands.

The teacher then said, "That's very interesting. The Gospel of Mark has only sixteen chapters. But at least I know that my lesson is going to hit its mark. Today I'm going to teach on what Jesus had to say about truthfulness."

Perhaps the greatest punishment for lying is not that a person gets caught in the lie, but rather, the hidden punishment that a liar can never truly believe what anyone else says.

Tell the truth! You'll suffer far less embarrassment and be much healthier emotionally. Even if truth-telling brings temporary pain, God delights in those who walk in integrity. He will honor your courage and bless you for doing the right thing.

A false witness shall not be unpunished,
and he that speaketh lies shall not escape.
Proverbs 19:5

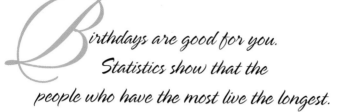

*Birthdays are good for you.
Statistics show that the
people who have the most live the longest.*

172

THERE once was a woman who, upon seeing her hair begin to turn gray, decided she must be getting old. She immediately slowed her pace, refused to wear bright colors, tried to act more sedate, and began to wear "sensible shoes." She put her hair up in a bun, wore long sleeves to cover what she was sure must be unsightly "old lady" arms, and could often be heard telling friends who asked how she was, "I suppose I'm doing as well as could expected for a person my age."

One day she overheard a teenager ask a friend, "How old is Miss Tilly?" The friend said, "Well, from the way she looks and acts, I'd say she's at least sixty-five or seventy." The woman was shocked they were talking about her—she was only fifty-five! She decided she was looking far too old for her years and immediately shifted into reverse. Bright colors, high heels, and more stylish clothes rejoined her closet. She cut her hair and used a rinse to cover the gray. Several months later, a forty-eight-year-old man asked her out and wouldn't believe her when she told him her age.

She concluded, "Fifty-five is a better speed limit than age limit."

So teach us to number our days, that we may apply our hearts unto wisdom.
Psalm 90:12

The only way to have a friend is to be one.

174

A YOUNG family in the 1950's had just purchased their first television set, so all the neighbors gathered to help them put up the antenna on the roof of their home. They weren't making much progress, though, since they had only the simplest of tools.

Then a new neighbor and his wife showed up with a large elaborate toolbox, filled with just about any gadget or tool one could imagine. They had everything needed to install the antenna, which was up in near-record time after their arrival.

The group of volunteers immediately went inside to see what kind of reception their neighbors would get on their new television set. The picture was crystal clear! They had done it!

As the neighbors stood around congratulating themselves on their fine work, they thanked their new neighbors for their valuable assistance. One of the women asked, "What is it that you make with such a well-equipped tool box?"

The new neighbors smiled sincerely and replied with genuine warmth, "Friends."

While you may not have a well-equipped toolbox, you certainly have a skill or attribute that would benefit someone else. Think about it. What "tools" can you use to make a new friend today?

A man that hath friends must shew himself friendly.
Proverbs 18:24

Hindsight explains the injury that foresight would have prevented.

THE mother of six children walked into her house one day to see all her children huddled together in a circle. She approached them to see what had evoked such intense interest, and she could hardly believe her eyes.

To her horror, in the middle of the circle of children were several baby skunks! She immediately screamed at the top of her voice, "Children! Run, run, run! Out, out, out!"

At the sound of their mother's alarmed voice, each child quickly grabbed a baby skunk and headed for the door. The screaming and panic, of course, set off the instinctual danger alarm in the skunks, and each of them quickly dispelled its horrible scent. Each child and the house itself were doused with an aroma that lingered for weeks, regardless of intense scrubbing and use of disinfectants.

How we react to a negative situation often has greater consequences than the initial situation we encounter! Don't make matters worse by jumping to conclusions and reacting based upon the emotions of the moment. Choose to act rather than to react, taking sufficient time to select a course of action based upon calm reason and common sense. And pray. God always has a ready answer.

Do not forsake wisdom, and she will protect you. . . .
When you walk, your steps will not be hampered;
when you run, you will not stumble.
Proverbs 4:6,12 NIV

I am defeated, and know it, if I meet any human being from whom I find myself unable to learn anything.

CARLOS Romulo, the former president of the Philippines, won an oratorical contest in the Manila high school he attended as a young man. His father was puzzled, however, when he saw his son ignore the congratulations of one of the other contestants. As they left the auditorium he asked, "Why didn't you shake hands with Julio?"

Carlos said, "I have no use for Julio. He was speaking ill of me before the contest." The father put his arm around his son and said, "Your grandfather used to tell me that the taller the bamboo grows, the lower it bends. Remember that always, my boy."

Every person has something to teach us, not only those who are experts in their fields or tell us what we want to hear. Each person is a living encyclopedia of ideas, insights, facts, experiences, and opinions.

A woman once advised a new employee: "Fifty percent of the people in this organization will teach you what to do and the other 50 percent what not to do. It's your challenge to figure out which percent goes with which person." Even if a person doesn't provide a good example, you can always learn from him or her what not to do!

A wise man will hear, and will increase learning; and a man of understanding shall attain unto wise counsels.

Proverbs 1:5

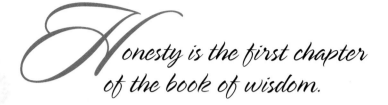

Honesty is the first chapter of the book of wisdom.

180

THE editor of the "weddings and engagements" section of a small-town newspaper grew tired of hearing from the town's citizens that she always embellished her reports of parties and celebrations. She decided that in the next issue she was going to tell the truth and see if she had greater favor with the citizenry. She wrote the following item:

"Married—Miss Sylvan Rhodes and Mr. James Collins, last Saturday at the Baptist parsonage, by the Rev. J. Gordon. The bride is a very ordinary town girl, who doesn't know any more about cooking than a jackrabbit and never helped her mother three days in her life. She is not a beauty by any means and has a gait like a duck. The groom is an up-to-date loafer. He has been living off the old folks at home all his life."

We may not always need to be so brutally honest! Truth, after all, is ultimately known only by God. He alone has the ability to see into the hearts of men and women and know everything involved in any situation or relationship.

We should be honest in expressing our hopes for another person's best welfare and success. That's a truth everybody loves to hear.

Provide things honest in the sight of all men.

Romans 12:17

A lot of people mistake a short memory for a clear conscience.

IN the 1890s a man drove by the farm of Mrs. John R. McDonald. A sudden gust of wind caught his black derby hat and whirled it onto the McDonald's property. He searched in vain for the hat and finally drove off bareheaded.

Mrs. McDonald retrieved the hat, and for the next forty-five years various members of her family wore it. Finally the old derby was beyond repair, completely worn out. It was at that point Mrs. McDonald went to the local newspaper and advertised for the owner of the hat. She noted in her ad that while the hat had been on the heads of the menfolk in her family, the hat had been on her conscience for forty-five years!

Is something nagging at your heart today—an awareness that you have committed a wrong against another person or a feeling that something has gone amiss in a relationship? Don't set aside those feelings. Seek to make amends.

A guilty conscience is a very heavy load to carry through life—one for which Jesus died on the cross. He did His part; now you do yours and obtain the freedom and peace He purchased for you!

*And herein do I exercise myself, to have always
a conscience void of offense toward God, and toward men.*
Acts 24:16

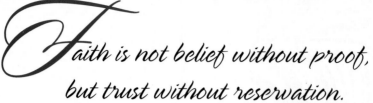

Faith is not belief without proof,
but trust without reservation.

DURING the terrible days of the Blitz in World War II, a father holding his young daughter by the hand ran from a building that had been struck by a bomb. In the front yard was a large hole left by a shell explosion several days before. Seeking shelter as quickly as possible, the father jumped into the hole and then held up his arms for his young daughter to follow.

Terrified at the explosions around her, yet unable to see her father in the darkness of the hole, she cried, "I can't see you, Papa!"

The father looked up against the sky, lit with white tracer lights and tinted red by burning buildings and called to his daughter, silhouetted at the hole's edge, "But I can see you, my darling. Jump!"

The little girl jumped, not because she could see her father, but because she trusted him to tell her the truth and to do what was best for her.

We may not be able to discern clearly where our Heavenly Father is leading us, but we can trust it is a good place. We may not know what God has "up His sleeve," but we can trust His arms to be everlasting.

I know whom I have believed, and am persuaded that he is able to keep that which I have committed unto him against that day.

2 Timothy 1:12

*A day hemmed in prayer
is less likely to unravel.*

186

IT was 2 A.M. when a weary traveler landed in Tahiti. Her flight from Hawaii had been a turbulent one, causing a delay in her arrival on the island. Her connecting flight to a nearby island had been canceled, forcing her to make plans to spend at least a day near the airport. An hour later, she found herself standing in a small motel room, totally exhausted after more than twenty-four hours of travel. As tired as she was however, her mind refused to stop racing with concern about whom to call and what to do.

The woman was on a short-term missionary trip to help set up a clinic on a remote South Seas island. Now she was beginning to wonder if she had heard God correctly! At that hour, and as weary as she was, she felt alone at the edge of the world. Glancing down at her watch, she saw it read 11 A.M.— the time her Bible Study group had said they would pray for her. *They're praying right now!* she thought, and suddenly, she felt peace. Within minutes, she was sound asleep.

When you feel as if you are about to unravel inside, turn to prayer. Prayer gives peace and helps us avoid danger.

Pray about everything. . . . If you do this you will experience God's peace. . . . His peace will keep your thoughts and your hearts quiet and at rest.

Philippians 4:6-7 TLB

When you flee temptations, don't leave a forwarding address.

SALLY was trying desperately to save all the pennies she could for the doll carriage she wanted to buy. She was turning in aluminum cans, offering to do extra chores—anything to make a few extra cents a week.

One night as she was saying her bedtime prayers, her mother overheard Sally praying, "O Lord, please help me to save my money for the doll carriage in Mr. Brown's store window. It's so beautiful and I want it so much. It's just right for my doll. And I'd be sure to let my friends play with it too."

Pleased at her daughter's prayer, Sally's mother was startled to hear the final line of the prayer.

"And please God, don't let the ice cream man come down our street this week!"

Just as we are each unique in our talents, abilities, background, and experiences, we are also unique in our temptations. What is tempting to one person may not be at all tempting to another.

Although the enemy of our souls knows our weaknesses, we know our Strength—Jesus. As we stick close to Him, when temptation comes, we can draw on His strength to turn from it.

*Now flee from youthful lusts, and pursue righteousness,
faith, love and peace, with those who call on
the Lord from a pure heart.*
2 Timothy 2:22 NASB

The past should be a springboard, not a hammock.

190

MANY people are good starters but poor finishers. When the going starts getting tough they listen to the little imp on their shoulder who whispers, "You can't do it" and "You'll never make it." Because of fear, many others do not even start.

What we must realize is that while doing something requires a risk, so does doing nothing. The risk of action may be failure, but the risks of inaction can be stagnation, dissatisfaction, and frustration—even loss to an evil enemy.

The story of the covered wagon crossing the plains toward the Golden West began with a song:

The Coward never started;

The Weak died on the way;

Only the Strong came through!

That's the way it is in life. But strength does not refer only to physical strength. True strength flows from the strong spirit—a spirit made powerful by a close relationship with God. He gives us the will and the tools we need to succeed, the dreams and the vision to show us the way, and the wisdom to turn any cursing into a blessing.

Lean on God for direction, and then continue to lean on Him for the wisdom and courage to finish what you've begun!

Forgetting the past and looking forward to what lies ahead, I strain to reach the end of the race and receive the prize.

Philippians 3:13-14 TLB

A teacher asked her pupils to tell the meaning of loving-kindness. A little boy jumped up and said, "Well, if I was hungry and someone gave me a piece of bread that would be kindness. But if they put a little jelly on it, that would be loving-kindness."

192

KINDNESS provides a house, but love makes a home. Kindness packs an adequate lunch, but love puts a note of encouragement inside.

Kindness provides a television set or computer as a learning aid, but love controls the remote control and cares enough to insist a child "sign off."

Kindness sends a child to bed on time, but love tucks the covers around a child's neck and gives a goodnight hug and kiss.

Kindness cooks a meal, but love selects from the "favorite foods" menu and lights the candles.

Kindness writes a thank-you note, but love thinks to include a joke or photograph or bookmark inside the envelope.

Kindness keeps a clean and tidy house, but love adds a bouquet of fresh flowers.

Kindness pours a glass of milk, but love occasionally adds a little chocolate syrup.

Kindness reads a bedtime story, but love uses all the funny voices.

Kindness makes sure homework is done, but love gives extra help with the difficult subjects.

Kindness is doing what is decent, basic, courteous, and necessary for an even, smooth, and gentle flow of life.

Love is taking the extra step to make life truly exciting, creative, and meaningful! Love is what makes things *special*.

Bless the LORD, O my soul. . . . who crowneth thee with lovingkindness and tender mercies; Who satisfieth thy mouth with good things.

Psalm 103:1, 4–5

Laughter is a tranquilizer with no side effects.

NORMAN Cousins was once asked by a group of physicians to meet with cancer patients at a hospital. He told how he had lost a quarter in a pay phone:

The operator said, "Sir, if you give me your name and address, we'll mail the coin to you."

He recited a full and long litany of all the steps and expense involved in returning his coin that way and concluded, "Now, operator, why don't you just return my coin and let's be friends?"

She repeated her offer and then asked if he had pushed the coin-return plunger. He hadn't, but when he did, the phone box spewed out close to four dollars worth of change!

The operator said, "Sir, will you please put the coins back in the box?"

Cousins replied, "If you give me your name and address I will be glad to mail you the coins."

The patients exploded with cheers as Cousins told his story. Then one of the physicians asked, "How many of you came into this room in pain?" More than half raised their hands. "How many of you in the past few minutes had less or no pain?" All nodded "yes."

Laughter: it's one of the best pain medications ever!

A merry heart doeth good like a medicine.
Proverbs 17:22

*God never asks
about our ability or
our inability—just our
availability.*

ONE of the items in *Ripley's Believe It or Not* is a picture of a plain bar of iron. It is valued at $5. The same bar of iron has a far different value, however, if it is fashioned into different items.

—As a pair of horse shoes, it would be worth $50.

—As sewing needles, it would be worth $5,000.

—As balance springs for fine Swiss watches, it would be worth $500,000.

The raw material is not what is important. What's important is how the raw material is developed!

Each of us has been given talents and abilities. Some have received more, others less, but all have received some unique gift from God. As Christians, we also enjoy spiritual gifts which flow from the Holy Spirit.

The value of these raw materials, however, is a moot point unless we develop and exercise our talents, abilities, and spiritual gifts as a force for divine good in this world.

If you don't know what your abilities and gifts are, ask God to reveal them to you. Then ask Him to show you what He wants you to do with them. Your happiness and success in life will be found in fulfilling His plan for your life.

I heard the voice of the Lord, saying, Whom shall I send,
and who will go for us? Then said I, Here am I; send me.
Isaiah 6:8

Whether you think you can or think you can't, you're right.

A NEW prison was built in British Columbia to replace the old prison, Fort Alcan, that had been used to house inmates for hundreds of years. After the prisoners were moved into their new quarters, they become part of a work crew to strip the old prison of lumber, electrical appliances, and plumbing that might be reused. Under the supervision of guards, the inmates began tearing down the old prison walls.

As they did, they were shocked at what they found. Although massive locks had sealed heavy metal doors and two-inch steel bars had covered the windows of the cells, the walls of the prison had actually been made out of paper and clay, painted to resemble iron! If any of the prisoners had given a mighty heave or hard kick against a wall, they might easily have knocked a hole in it, allowing for escape. For years, however, they had huddled in their locked cells, regarding escape as impossible.

Nobody had ever *tried* to escape, because they thought it was impossible.

Many people today are prisoners of fear. They never attempt to pursue their dreams because the thought of reaching them seems impossible. But how do you know you can't succeed if you don't try?

As he thinketh in his heart, so is he.

Proverbs 23:7

The best way to cheer yourself up is to cheer up somebody else.

A GRIEF-STRICKEN mother sat in a hospital room in stunned silence, tears streaming down her cheeks. She had just lost her only child. She gazed into space as the head nurse asked her, "Did you notice the little boy sitting in the hall just outside?"

The nurse continued, "His mother was brought here from their poor one-room apartment. The two of them came to this country only three months ago, because all their family members had been killed in war. They don't know anyone here.

"That little boy has been sitting outside his mother's room every day for a week in hopes his mother would come out of her coma."

By now the woman was listening intently.

"Fifteen minutes ago his mother died. It's my job to tell him that, at age seven, he is all alone in the world—there's nobody who even knows his name." The nurse paused and then asked, "I don't suppose you would tell him for me?"

The woman stood, dried her tears, and went out to the boy. She put her arms around the homeless child and invited him to come with her to her childless home. In the darkest hour of both their lives, they became lights to each other.

Give, and it shall be given unto you.
Luke 6:38

Failure isn't falling down. It's staying down.

IN 1991, Anne Busquet was General Manager of the Optima Card division for American Express. When five of her 2,000 employees were found to have hidden $24 million in losses, she was held accountable. Busquet had to face the fact that, as an intense perfectionist, she apparently came across as intimidating and confrontational to her subordinates to the point they were more willing to lie than to report bad news to her!

Busquet lost her Optima job but was given a second chance by American Express: An opportunity to salvage one of its smaller businesses. Her self-esteem shaken, she nearly turned down the offer. Then she decided this was her chance to change the way she related to others. She took on the new job as a personal challenge.

Realizing she had to be much more understanding, she began to work on being more patient and listening more carefully and intently. She learned to solicit bad news in an unintimidating way.

Four years after she was removed from her previous position, Anne Busquet was promoted to be an executive vice president at American Express.

Failure is not the end; it is an opportunity to train for a new beginning and a better life!

A just man falleth seven times, and riseth up again.
Proverbs 24:16

Nobody can make you feel inferior without your consent.

THREE women on a hike came upon an unlocked cabin deep in the woods. Receiving no response to their knocks, they went inside to find one room, simply furnished. Nothing seemed unusual except that the large, potbellied, cast iron stove was hung from the ceiling, suspended in midair by wires.

The psychologist said, "It is obvious this lonely trapper has elevated his stove so he can curl up under it and experience a return to the womb." The engineer responded, "Nonsense! This is thermodynamics! He has found a way to distribute heat more evenly in his cabin." The theologian interrupted, "I'm sure this has religious meaning. Fire 'lifted up' has been a religious symbol for millennia."

As the three debated, the cabin owner returned. The hikers immediately asked him why the stove was hung from the ceiling. He replied succinctly, "I had plenty of wire, but not much stove pipe."

Others may try to second-guess your motives, downplay your ideas, or insult you, but only *you* know why you do what you do, what you think and feel, and how you relate to God.

Stay true to who you are in Christ Jesus!

I am fearfully and wonderfully made.
Psalm 139:14

Acknowledgments

The publisher would like to honor and acknowledge the following for the quotes used in this book:

Ruth Bell Graham (6), Jean Hodges (8), Henry Ward Beecher (12), Joseph Addison (14), Cyrus (16), Betty Mills (22), Josh Billings (24), Thackeray (26), Joyce Heinrich and Annette La Placa (28), St. Basil (30), Mother Teresa (32, 168), Catherine Graham (60), Lillian Dickson (62), Cervantes (64), Mark Twain (66, 154), William James (68), Zig Ziglar (70), Bill Cosby (72), Euripedes (76), William Carey (78), Benjamin Franklin (80), Mary Gardner Brainard (88), Richard Exley (146), John Newton (148), Mark Steele (150), Dr. John Olson (164), Reverend Larry Lorenzoni (172), Ralph Waldo Emerson (174), George Herbert Palmer (178), Thomas Jefferson (180), Doug Larsen (182), Elton Trueblood (184), Ivern Ball (190), Merceline Cox (194), Henry Ford (198), Mary Pickford (202), Eleanor Roosevelt (204).

Additional copies of this book are available
from your local bookstore.

God's Little Devotional Book—Special Gift Edition
God's Little Devotional Bible
God's Little Devotional Bible for Women
God's Little Devotional Book for Moms
God's Little Book of Promises for Mothers
God's Little Devotional Book on Prayer

Honor Books
Tulsa, Oklahoma